AQA GCSE
FOUNDATION PLUS
Homework Book

Claire Turpin

About this book
This book provides extra exercises for the topics covered in the Foundation Plus Student Book. There are four or five exercises for each Student Book chapter. In each, the first exercise (HW1) reviews topics from previous chapters; the final exercise reviews the chapter and includes some exam-style questions. The remaining two or three exercises for each chapter give extra practice in the key topics.

Contents

Unit 1
N1	Integers and decimals	1-4
D1	Probability	5-10
N2	Decimal calculations	11-14
D2	Collecting data	15-19
N3	Fractions, decimals and percentages 1	20-23
D3	Displaying and interpreting data	24-27
N4	Ratio and proportion	28-31
D4	Averages charts	32-36

Unit 2
A1	Linear graphs	37-40
N5	Integers, powers and roots	41-44
A2	Expressions	45-48
A3	Real-life graphs	49-53
A4	Sequences	54-57
N6	Fractions, decimals and percentages 2	58-61
A5	Equations 1	62-75
A6	Formulae and inequalities	66-70

Unit 3
G1	Length and area	71-74
G2	2D shapes	75-79
G3	3D shapes	80-83
N7	Proportionality	84-86
G4	Transformations	87-91
G5	2D and 3D shapes	92-96
A7	Equations 2	97-100
G6	Constructions and loci	101-105
G7	Further geometry	106-110

OXFORD
UNIVERSITY PRESS

OXFORD
UNIVERSITY PRESS

Great Clarendon Street, Oxford OX2 6DP

Oxford University Press is a department of the University of Oxford.
It furthers the University's objective of excellence in research,
scholarship,and education by publishing worldwide in

Oxford   New York

Auckland   Cape Town   Dar es Salaam   Hong Kong   Karachi
Kuala Lumpur   Madrid   Melbourne   Mexico City   Nairobi
New Delhi   Shanghai   Taipei   Toronto

With offices in

Argentina   Austria   Brazil   Chile   Czech Republic   France   Greece
Guatemala   Hungary   Italy   Japan   Poland   Portugal   Singapore
South Korea   Switzerland   Thailand   Turkey   Ukraine   Vietnam

© Oxford University Press

The moral rights of the author have been asserted

Database right Oxford University Press (maker)

First published 2011

All rights reserved. No part of this publication may be reproduced,
stored in a retrieval system, or transmitted, in any form or by any
means, without the prior permission in writing of Oxford University
Press, or as expressly permitted by law, or under terms agreed
with the appropriate reprographics rights organization. Enquiries
concerning reproduction outside the scope of the above should
be sent to the Rights Department, Oxford University Press, at the
address above

You must not circulate this book in any other binding or cover
and you must impose this same condition on any acquirer

British Library Cataloguing in Publication Data

Data available

ISBN 978 0 19 912896-9

10 9 8 7 6 5 4 3 2

Printed in Great Britain by Bell and Bain Ltd., Glasgow

Cover photo: Nicemonkey/Dreamstime

MIX
Paper from
responsible sources
FSC® C007785
www.fsc.org

N1 HW1 Check-in review

1 Look at these number cards.

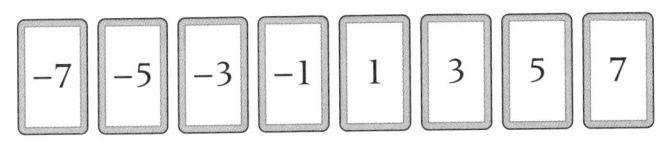

$\boxed{-7}$ $\boxed{-5}$ $\boxed{-3}$ $\boxed{-1}$ $\boxed{1}$ $\boxed{3}$ $\boxed{5}$ $\boxed{7}$

   a Choose two cards that add to 2. −1 + 3
   b Choose two cards that add to −8. −7 + −1
   c Choose any four cards that add to make 0.
   d What is the total of adding all eight cards?

2 a Here are three number cards.

$\boxed{5}$ $\boxed{8}$ $\boxed{2}$

   Show that the mean of these numbers is 5.   5 + 8 + 2 = 15
   15 ÷ 3 = 5

   b The mean of three numbers is 4.
   One of these numbers is 3.
   i What could the other numbers be?
   ii What else could the numbers be?
   Use different numbers from your answer to part **i**.

3 When n is 6, work out the value of $2(n + 3)$.
   2 × 6 = 12 ~~in 2 work~~ + 6 = 18

4 The diagram shows four identical white rectangles
   (8 cm by 3 cm) around a shaded square.
   What is the area of the square?

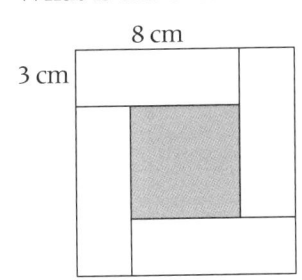

   8 cm
   3 cm

   8 × 3 = 24

N1 HW2 Place value and reading scales

1 a Write each of these numbers in words.

  i 567   **ii** 11 567   **iii** 345 004
  iv 120 001 **v** 3450.03   **vi** 3 001 003

b Write each of these numbers in figures.

  i One hundred thousand
  ii Thirty-two thousand and four
  iii One million and twenty-six
  iv Twenty-two thousand and twenty point four
  v One hundred thousand point zero five.

2 Use the information given to work out each of these calculations without using a calculator.

  a 34 × 45 = 1530   What is 3.4 × 45?
  b 94 × 49 = 4606   What is 94 × 4.9?
  c 28 × 35 = 980   What is 2.8 × 3.5?
  d 78 × 27 = 2106   What is 0.78 × 27?
  e 56 × 29 = 1624   What is 5600 × 29?

3 Write the number that each of the arrows is pointing to.

a (scale from 40 to 70, marked at 50, 60, 65)

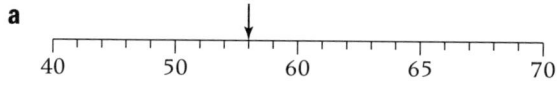

b (scale from 4 to 6, marked at 5)

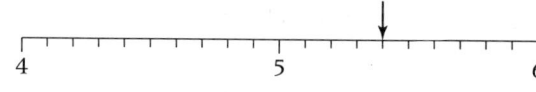

c (scale from 14 to 15)

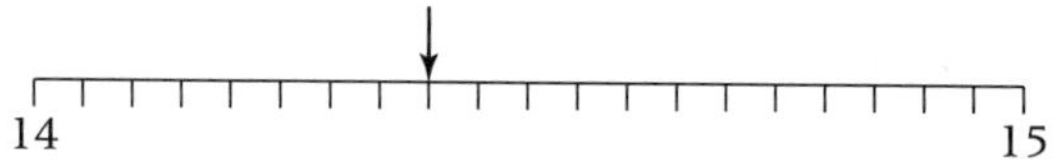

4 Here is the Fowey–St Austell bus timetable.

Fowey	11.10	11.40
Tywardreath	11.22	11.52
Par	11.29	11.59
St Blazey	11.36	12.06
St Austell	11.58	12.28

  a How long does the 11.22 bus from Tywardreath take to get to St Austell?
  b Between which two towns does the journey take the longest?

N1 HW3 Negative numbers

1 Write these numbers in order starting with the smallest.
  a −4, 9, 0, −6, 12, −15
  b −1, 1, 5, −9, 3, 10
  c 12, 3, −2, 3, 0, −4
  d −5, 10, −35, 13, 3, 20
  e 0, −10, 9, 3, −5, −20
  f −100, 30, 0, −29, 39, 12

2 Find the number that lies exactly halfway between these pairs of numbers.
  a −3 and 3   b −5 and 3   c −10 and −6
  d −12 and 10   e −3 and 5   f −4.5 and 0.5

3 Calculate
  a $4 - 5$ b $-3 + 4$ c $-4 + -5$
  d $15 - 18$ e $14 - -4$ f $-4 - -3$
  g $-3 + 15$ h $-10 - 3$ i $14 + -14$
  j $-8 - -3$ k $-7 + -4$ l $6 + -6$
  m -4×5 n 9×-3 o -11×0
  p -5×-4 q 10×-5 r -4×-4
  s 5×-3 t -6×-6 u $-96 \div 12$
  v -12×-12 w $-99 \div 3$ x -24×8

4 Choose a number card to make each of these calculations correct.

  | −4 | −2 | 2 | 5 | −5 | 4 |

  a $2 \times \square = -4$ b $4 \div \square = -2$
  c $\square \times 5 = 25$ d $\square \div -5 = 1$
  e $-2 \div \square = \frac{1}{2}$ f $\square \times -4 = 8$
  g $\square \div 2 = -2$ h $-5 \times \square = -20$

N1 HW4 Chapter review

1 a Use the information that

17 × 16 = 272

to write the value of
  a 1.7 × 16
  b 1.7 × 1.6
  c 27.2 ÷ 1600

2 Round each of these numbers to the nearest
  i 2 sf **ii** 3 sf
  a 5.269   **b** 26.392
  c 0.3994 **d** 0.006 116

3 There are p cereal bars in a box
  a Write the number of cereal bars in
    i 2 boxes **ii** 10 boxes **iii** y boxes
  b Ranee opens a box and eats two cereal bars.
  Write an expression for the number of cereal bars left in the box.

4 Jordan wrote the temperatures at different times on 1st February 2005.

  a What was
    i the highest temperature
    ii the lowest temperature?

Time	Temperature in °C
Midnight	−7
5 am	−10
11 am	1
4 pm	6
9 pm	−2

  b Work out the difference in the temperature between
    i midnight and 5 am
    ii 5 am and 4 pm.

  At 11 pm the temperature has fallen by 4 °C from its value at 9 pm.

  c Work out the temperature at 11 pm.

D1 HW1 Check-in review

1. Write each of these numbers in figures.
   a Three thousand and four
   b Forty-five thousand and six
   c Ninety thousand and ten
   d Nine million, two thousand and four hundred.

2. Write each of these numbers in words.
   a 7500
   b 217 800
   c 95 012
   d 707 007
   e 990 909
   f 7 048 003

3. Round each of these numbers to the given degree of accuracy.
   a 3495 (nearest 100)
   b 34.89 (1 decimal place)
   c 1234 (nearest 10)
   d 0.9847 (2 decimal places)
   e 19.834 55 (3 decimal places)
   f 3 298 000 (1 significant figure)
   g 3.998 (2 significant figures)
   h 12 986 (nearest 100)
   i 12.0001 (3 decimal places)

4. Calculate
   a $7 - 11$
   b $-6 + 7$
   c $-6 + -7$
   d $12 - 24$
   e $14 - -7$
   f $-6 - -11$
   g $-8 + 35$
   h $-19 - 8$
   i -4×12
   j 7×-7
   k -6×0
   l -12×-3
   m 14×-7
   n -6×-9
   o 7×-11
   p -9×-6
   q -3×2
   r -13×-6

D1 HW2 Probability and the probability scale

1 A fair dice, numbered 1–6, is rolled. Calculate the probability that the dice will land on

- **a** a 6
- **b** an odd number
- **c** a square number
- **d** a cube number
- **e** a prime number
- **f** a multiple of 3
- **g** a factor of 12
- **h** a 7.

2 A bag of sweets contains these flavours:

4 strawberry
3 orange
2 blackcurrant
5 lemon

Calculate the probability of picking

- **a** an orange sweet
- **b** a lemon sweet
- **c** a raspberry sweet.

3 The letters of the word MATHEMATICS are put into a bag. One letter is taken out at random.
Calculate the probability that the letter is

- **a** an M
- **b** not an M
- **c** a vowel
- **d** a consonant
- **e** not an A
- **f** a B.

4 The possible outcomes in a football match are win, lose or draw. The probability that Fowey Town Football Club win, lose or draw is shown in this table.

Outcome	Win	Lose	Draw
Probability	0.65	0.25	?

- **a** Calculate the probability that Fowey Town will draw.
- **b** What is the most likely outcome?

D1 HW3 Mutually exclusive outcomes

1 Richard has a bag of sweets. He picks one sweet out at random. The probability that the sweet is a particular colour is

Colour	Red	Green	Yellow	Orange	Purple
Probability	$\frac{1}{5}$	$\frac{1}{20}$	$\frac{3}{10}$	$\frac{15}{100}$	?

a Calculate the probability of picking a sweet that is

i purple ii blue.

b If there are 40 sweets in the bag, how many of them are each colour?

2 The two-way table shows the number of students in a class who are left- and right-handed.

	Left-handed	Right-handed
Boy	4	12
Girl	3	9

a How many left-handed students are there in the class?
b A student is selected at random. Calculate the probability they will be

i a boy   ii a left-handed girl   iii a right-handed boy.

3 A spinner with the numbers 10, 11, 12, 13, 14, 15, 16, 17 is spun. Calculate the probability that the spinner will land on

a an even number
b a prime number
c a multiple of 3
d a factor of 30
e a square number
f a multiple of 3 and 5
g not a prime number
h a multiple of 9
i a cube number.

D1 HW4 Two-way tables and expected frequency

1 A box of chocolates contains milk and plain chocolates. Some of these chocolates contain nuts. The two-way table shows the number of chocolates in each category.

	Milk chocolate	Plain chocolate
Contains nuts	5	7
Does not contain nuts	12	8

One chocolate is selected at random.

Calculate the probability that the chocolate is a

a plain chocolate that contains nuts
b milk chocolate
c chocolate that contains nuts
d plain chocolate
e milk chocolate that contains nuts

2 Students at a school play either hockey, football or rugby. The two-way table shows information about these students.

	Hockey	Football	Rugby	Total
Male	14			45
Female		25	7	
Total	29	56		

a Copy and complete the two-way table.
b How many students were in the class?
c Calculate the probability that a student chosen at random is a

  i hockey player
  ii male and a football player
  iii female
  iv female and a rugby player

3 If a dice is rolled 300 times, how many times would you expect it to land on

a a 6
b an even number
c a factor of 8
d an 8?

4 The probability of Zahir being early or on time for work is 0.76.

a Calculate the probability of his being late for work.
b Over 300 work days, how many times would you expect him to be late for work?

D1 HW5 Two events

1 Laura's journey to work takes her through two sets of traffic lights. When she arrives at each set of lights they are both equally likely to be showing red, amber or green.

  a Copy and complete this table to show all nine possible outcomes.
  b Copy and complete this tree diagram to show all nine possible outcomes.
  c Calculate the probability of finding both sets of lights on
   i red
   ii different colours
   iii the same colour.
  d Laura travels to work 180 times in a year. How often can she expect both sets of lights to be on red?

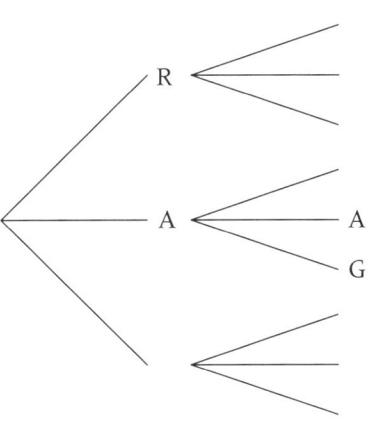

		Second lights		
		R	A	G
First lights	R		RA	
	A			
	G			

2 Tomasz tosses two coins and records whether he gets heads or tails.
  a Show all the possible results in a table.
  b Show all the possible results in a tree diagram.

Tomasz repeats the coin tossing 100 times.

  c How often should Tomasz expect to get
   i two heads
   ii a head and a tail, in any order
   iii two tails?
  d Tomasz actually gets two heads 45 times. Do you think the coins are fair? Explain your answer.

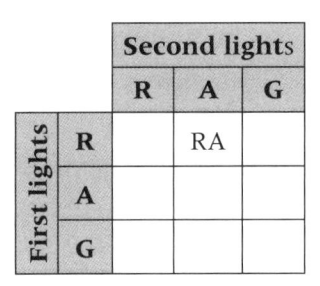

D1 HW6 Chapter review

1 A spinner is numbered 1 to 5.
Dale spins the spinner and throws a coin.

  a List all the possible outcomes.
  The spinner is biased.

Number	1	2	3	4	5
Probability	0.34	0.2	0.1	0.25	?

  b Work out the probability that the spinner will land on
  i 5 **ii** 6.
  c Work out the probability that the spinner will land on an even number.

2 22 coloured balls are used to play a game of snooker.
15 of them are red and the rest have different colours.
One of the balls is chosen at random.
Write the probability that the ball chosen will be

  a red   **b** not red.

3 A packet contains 9 green counters and 6 blue counters.
A counter is taken from the packet at random.

  a Write the probability that

  i a green counter will be taken
  ii a yellow counter will not be taken.

  b Write all the possible outcomes of taking two counters from the packet.

4 A fair coin is tossed and a fair dice is thrown.

  a Copy and complete the sample space diagram to show all possible outcomes.

		Dice					
		1	2	3	4	5	6
Coin	Head						
	Tail			Tail, 3			

  b Calculate the probability of getting

  i a 6 and a Head   **ii** a prime number and a Tail.

N2 HW1 Check-in review

1 A dice is to be thrown.
The probability that this dice will land on each of the numbers 1 to 6 is given in the table.

Number	1	2	3	4	5	6
Probability	x	0.1	0.3	0.2	0.2	0.1

The dice is to be thrown once.

a Calculate the value of x.

b Calculate the probability that the dice will land on a number higher than 4.

The dice is thrown 500 times.

c Estimate the number of times the dice is likely to land on a six.

2 Round each number to the given degree of accuracy.

a 6795 (nearest 100)
b 45.45 (1 decimal place)
c 1564 (nearest 10)
d 0.6769 (2 decimal places)
e 2564 (2 significant figures)
f 59.635 65 (3 decimal places)
g 6 567 000 (1 significant figure)
h 15.78 (1 decimal place)
i 6.998 (2 significant figures)
j 15 676 (nearest 100)
k 0.000 566 4 (3 significant figures)
l 16.0056 (3 decimal places)

3 A pencil is of length 12 cm, measured to the nearest centimetre.
A pencil case is of length 12.1 cm, measured to the nearest millimetre.
Explain why it might not be possible for the pencil to fit in the pencil case.

N2 HW2 Written and mental calculations

1 Use a written method to work out

   a 54.6 + 74.3   **b** 12.65 + 7.32   **c** 18.34 + 8.45
   d 16.7 − 3.6   **e** 13.95 − 2.24   **f** 9.78 − 3.47
   g 143.4 + 5.8   **h** 74.68 + 54.9   **i** 3.667 + 6.418
   j 98.46 − 49.54   **k** 69.735 − 14.856   **l** 35.67 − 29.7

2 Use a mental or written method to work out each of the problems.

   a Karen sells fish. On Monday she sells 81.4 kg and on Tuesday she sells 66.7 kg. How much fish has Karen sold altogether?
   b A bucket full of sand weighs 19.5 kg. The bucket weighs 1.65 kg. How much does the sand weigh?
   c James is saving his money in his money box. In July he has £64.36. In August he has £56.95. How much money did James save in August?
   d Paula is training to run a marathon. During 4 days of training she runs the following distances: 18.5 miles, 21.95 miles, 11.3 miles and 26.27 miles. Work out the total distance she runs during the 4 days.

3 Use an appropriate method to calculate these. Write each method you have used.

   a 34 × 100   **b** 28 × 4   **c** 19 × 6
   d 214 ÷ 4   **e** 624 ÷ 8   **f** 12.6 × 21
   g 54.8 × 20   **h** 336 ÷ 6   **i** 26.5 × 5
   j 3.45 × 2.5   **k** 34 × 2.8   **l** 15 × 0.3

4 Use an appropriate method to work out each of these problems.

   a 15 × 46 = 690. What is 15 × 4.6?
   b 1 litre of petrol costs 129.4p. How much does 43 litres of petrol cost?
   c Sonia buys 32 chocolate bars that cost £9.28. How much does each bar cost?
   d Lawson drinks 2.75 litres of water every day. How much water does he drink in 2 weeks?

N2 HW3 Order of operations and estimation

1 Copy each of these calculations and insert brackets, where necessary, to make each statement correct. Not every statement needs brackets.

   a $4 + 3 \times 4 = 28$
   b $6 \div 4 - 1 = 2$
   c $7 \times 2 + 8 \div 4 = 16$
   d $3^2 - 4 \times 2 + 6 = 40$
   e $60 \times 2^2 - 1 = 180$
   f $3 + 2 \times 9 = 45$
   g $5 + 20 \div 4 = 10$
   h $4^2 + 3 \times 2 = 38$
   i $3 \times 2 + 4 \times 6 = 30$

2 Work out these calculations.

   a $5 + 4 \times 5$
   b $10 + 2 \times 6 + 3$
   c $4 + 2 \times (4 + 5)$
   d $4^2 - 10 \div 2$
   e $12 \div 3 - 2 \times 2$
   f $(5 + 16) \div 3$
   g $8 + 4^3 \times 2$
   h $3 \times (5 - 3) + 1$
   i $80 \div 2^3 + 3 \times 8$
   j $\dfrac{6 + 4 \times 4}{11}$
   k $\dfrac{4 \times 5 + 2}{2}$
   l $\dfrac{81}{2^2 + 5}$

Example

Work out these mentally.   a 16×0.2 b $24 \div 0.02$

a $16 \times 0.2 = 16 \times 2 \times 0.1 = 32 \times 0.1 = 3.2$
b $24 \div 0.02 = 24 \div 2 \div 0.01 = 12 \div 0.01 = 1200$

---

3 Work out these calculations using a mental method. Show your method.

   a 4×0.02
   b $32 \div 0.8$
   c 1.6×0.4
   d $6 \div 0.03$
   e $2.1 \div 0.07$

4 Write a suitable estimate for each of these calculations. In each case clearly show how you estimated your answer.

   a $\dfrac{39.9 \times 21.5}{1.98^3}$
   b $\dfrac{47.9 \times 9.8^2}{0.49 \times 21.56}$
   c $\sqrt{98.7 \div 1.98}$
   d $\{2.6^2 + (4.57 - 0.62)\}^2$
   e $\dfrac{219 + (3.98 + 16.08)^2}{\sqrt{74.5 \div 2.11}}$

N2 HW4 Chapter review

1. David takes 38 boxes out of his van. The weight of each box is 25.6 kg. Work out the **total** weight of the 38 boxes.

   $25.6 \times 38 = 972.8 kg$

2. Use a written method to work these out.

   a 17×25 b 24×16 c 45×347
   d $318 \div 6$ e $504 \div 9$ f $208 \div 16$
   g 7.6×6 h 17×7.5 i 3.74×18
   j $112.5 \div 9$ k $63.6 \div 12$ l $29.25 \div 9$

3. For each of these give a suitable estimate. Show your workings clearly.

   a 9.74×4.98 b $92.7 \div 6.12$

   c $\dfrac{12.94 \times 9.94}{5.87}$ d $\dfrac{78.9 \times 29.99}{25.4}$

4. Monique goes to the shops and buys

   5kg of potatoes at £0.45 per kg
   1.54kg of apples at £1.99 per kg
   0.5kg of tomatoes at £0.88 per kg
   2.2kg of bananas at £0.85 per kg
   1.5kg of carrots at £0.68 per kg
   0.785kg of cherries at £8.99 per kg
   0.61kg of grapes at £1.87 per kg
   4 avocados at £0.67 each

   a Work out the total cost of the shopping.
   b Work out the change she would receive from a £20 note.

5. Work out
   $64 \div 4(5^2 - 23)$

D2 HW1 Check-in review

1 A fair dice is rolled and a spinner is spun.
One possible outcome is (6, blue).

a Copy and complete the sample space diagram to show all possible outcomes.

		Dice					
		1	2	3	4	5	6
Spinner	Blue						6, blue
	Red						
	Green						
	Yellow						

b Calculate the probability of getting

  i a 6 and a blue
  ii a prime number and a red
  iii a factor of 12 and a yellow
  iv a square number with any colour.

2 Write these numbers in words.
  a 67 000   **b** 40 007
  c 687 900   **d** 11 000 000
  e 4 600 007   **f** 699 999

3 The probability that a new car is faulty is 0.09.
Calculate the probability that it is not faulty.

4 Samira does a statistical experiment. She throws a dice 600 times. She scores six 150 times.
Is the dice fair? Explain your answer.

D2 HW2 Frequency tables and data collection

1 Asma did a survey to find out the number of brothers and sisters the students have in her class. The results were

4	2	2	0	1	3	0	0	2
2	3	4	1	4	2	0	2	1
1	0	5	2	2	1	0	4	1

a Draw a tally chart to show this information.

Number of brothers and sisters	Tally	Number of students
0		
1		

b How many students have more than 3 brothers and sisters?

c Calculate how many brothers and sisters the class have in total.

2 These results show how many TVs students' families own.

Number of TVs	0	1	2	3	4	5
Number of students	1	7	12	13	5	1

a How many students were included in the survey?

b Calculate the total number of TVs owned by all of the students.

3 The number of A levels students obtained are

1	3	3	3	2	3	4	3	2
3	3	1	2	2	4	3	2	2
0	1	2	2	3	3	4	3	3

a Is this data collection an observation, a controlled experiment or data logging?

b Draw a suitable data collection sheet for these data.

c Write the most common number of A levels achieved.

d Calculate the total number of A levels achieved.

4 a Describe what is meant by a **random sample**.

b Explain why choosing 15 of your friends to complete a survey is not a random sample.

D2 HW3 Surveys, questionnaires and grouped data

1 Jimmy surveys people about their personal fitness.
One question in his questionnaire is
How often do you keep fit?
Not very often ☐ *Sometimes* ☐ *Quite often* ☐ *Lots* ☐
  a Write two criticisms of the question.
  b Write a better question.

2 a Devise a question that could have given these data.

Colour	Number of students
Red	3
Light Brown	15
Black	2
Blonde	9
Grey	3

  b Calculate the total number of students in the survey.
  c Make one criticism of the choices of categories for the colour.

3 Decide whether these data are discrete or continuous.
  a The height of students in your class.
  b The shoe size of students in your class.
  c The time it takes to walk to school.
  d The weight of new born babies.
  e The number a dice lands on when tossed 30 times.

4 The heights of students in a class, in metres, are

  1.60 1.45 1.51 1.63 1.70 1.46 1.38 1.44
  1.52 1.39 1.50 1.48 1.60 1.52 1.36 1.70
  1.63 1.55 1.49 1.36 1.45 1.42 1.51 1.67

  a Draw and complete a frequency table, using class intervals $1.35 < h \leq 1.40$, $1.40 < h \leq 1.45$, etc.
  b Which class interval has the most common height?
  c Explain why 1.50 metres cannot be put in the class interval $1.50 < h \leq 1.55$

D2 HW4 Random sampling and two events

1 a Decide whether each of these methods is random.
  i Selecting the first student from a register.
  ii Putting everyone's name into a hat and picking one.
  iii Selecting your closest friend.
  iv Number all students from 1–99 and roll a 0–9 dice twice to generate a 2-digit number.
  b Describe a method of random sampling that is different to any method described in part **a**.

2 Sonia wants to buy a new house. She has created a database of the six houses she is considering buying.

House	Price in £	Location	Number of bedrooms	Garden	Garage	Good condition?
1	250 000	City	3	Big	No	Yes
2	169 000	Town	3	None	No	Yes
3	213 500	Rural	2	Small	No	Yes
4	299 000	Rural	3	Big	Yes	No
5	175 000	Town	2	Big	Yes	No
6	325 000	Rural	4	Big	No	Yes

  a Which house is the cheapest with the fewest bedrooms?
  b Which house is the most expensive with 3 bedrooms?
  c Sonia wants a house in a rural location, with at least 3 bedrooms and with a big garden. She would also prefer to have a garage if possible. Which house would give her all of these things?

3 This two-way table shows the number of students at Mansfield School who play hockey and football.

	Hockey	Football
Male	9	55
Female	23	32

  a Calculate the number of
    i female students **ii** hockey players.
  b Calculate as fractions, the proportion of students
    i who are male and hockey players **ii** who are female.

D2 HW5 Chapter review

1. Class 10B study either French, Spanish or Italian. The two-way table shows this information.

	French	Spanish	Italian	Total
Male		12		
Female	12		6	22
Total	26		14	

   a Complete the two-way table.
   b How many students were in the class?

2. 50 students have to choose to go to the theatre, the art gallery or the science museum.
   23 of the students are boys.
   8 of the boys choose to visit the theatre.
   9 of the girls choose to visit the art gallery.
   13 of the boys choose to visit the science museum.
   17 of the students choose to visit the theatre.

	Theatre	Art Gallery	Science Museum	Total
Male				
Female				
Total				

   a Copy and complete the two-way table.
   b How many boys chose to go to the art gallery?

3. Here is a record of the heights, in cm, of pea plants.

   21 22 11 16 22 13 11 25 9 17 21 24 27
   25 12 14 8 12 6 17 19 26 26 18 21 13
   23 7 12 26 14 8 12 26 17 19 23 29 21

   a Copy and complete the frequency table.

Height, h, cm	Tally	Frequency
$5 < h \leq 10$		
$10 < h \leq 15$		
$15 < h \leq 20$		
$20 < h \leq 25$		
$25 < h \leq 30$		

   b How many pea plants were over 20 cm tall?
   c What was the most common height for the pea plants?

N3 HW1 Check-in review

1 A bag contains 5 grey balls, 2 white balls and 3 black balls.

One ball is taken out of the bag and then replaced.
Calculate the probability that the ball is

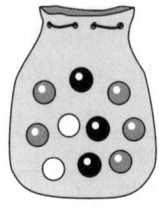

  a white
  b black
  c grey
  d red.
  e If you were to take out a ball and then replace it 200 times, how many times would you expect to get a white ball?

2 Use an appropriate method of calculation to work out

  a 16×43
  b 15×54
  c 23×466
  d $184 \div 4$
  e $203 \div 7$
  f $375 \div 15$
  g 7.6×4
  h 17×6.5
  i 1.74×13
  j $32.76 \div 9.1$
  k $59.52 \div 6.4$
  l $99.54 \div 7.9$

3 Derek recorded the heights, in cm, of the plants in his garden.

11	22	21	6	22	13	11	25	9	17	21	24	17
25	22	14	28	12	6	27	19	26	26	29	11	23
8	7	22	16	14	8	12	26	17	19	13	29	21

  a Copy and complete the frequency table for these data.

Height, h, cm	Tally	Frequency
$5 < h \leqslant 10$		
$10 < h \leqslant 15$		
$15 < h \leqslant 20$		
$20 < h \leqslant 25$		
$25 < h \leqslant 30$		

  b How many plants were over the height of 15 cm?
  c What was the most common height for the plants?

N3 HW2 Fractions, decimals and percentages

1 a Cancel each of these fractions into their simplest form.

   i $\frac{2}{10}$ ii $\frac{5}{45}$ iii $\frac{20}{30}$ iv $\frac{40}{55}$
   v $\frac{15}{25}$ vi $\frac{27}{81}$ vii $\frac{14}{49}$ viii $\frac{48}{64}$

b Copy and complete these equivalent fractions.

   i $\frac{1}{2} = \frac{?}{16}$ ii $\frac{6}{7} = \frac{24}{?}$ iii $\frac{5}{9} = \frac{?}{81}$
   iv $\frac{6}{13} = \frac{?}{65}$ v $\frac{24}{32} = \frac{6}{?}$ vi $\frac{5}{75} = \frac{1}{?}$

2 Use a suitable method to calculate

   a $\frac{3}{11}$ of £33   **b** $\frac{5}{7}$ of 350 kg   **c** $\frac{7}{9}$ of 63p
   d $\frac{11}{20}$ of 100 g   **e** $\frac{9}{15}$ of 45°   **f** $\frac{14}{25}$ of €600
   g $\frac{5}{6}$ of $300   **h** $\frac{6}{13}$ of £104   **i** $\frac{1}{6}$ of 192 people
   j $\frac{1}{20}$ of 500 people   **k** $\frac{7}{12}$ of 168 cm   **l** $\frac{9}{11}$ of 572 miles

3 Write these numbers in order of size.
Start with the smallest number first.

   a 0.5, 22%, $\frac{3}{10}$, 0.45, $\frac{2}{5}$ **b** $\frac{4}{7}$, 55%, $\frac{5}{11}$, 0.52, $\frac{1}{2}$
   c $\frac{7}{12}$, 62%, 0.54, $\frac{2}{3}$, 0.6   **d** $\frac{3}{4}$, $\frac{7}{9}$, 0.77, $\frac{7}{13}$, 80%

4 a Find these percentages without using a calculator.
You must show all of your workings.

   i   50% of £400   ii   25% of £200
   iii   10% of £60   iv   1% of 600p
   v   30% of €550   vi   20% of $350
   vii 40% of 90p   viii 15% of $800
   ix   55% of 1800 g   x   75% of 860 kg
   xi   35% of €180   xii 13% of 40 cm

b Use a suitable method to calculate these. Where appropriate round your answers to 2 decimal places.

   i   25% of £49   ii   17.5% of 67 m
   iii   34% of $458   iv   12% of 740 tonnes
   v   98% of 58 kg   vi   89% of 2550 mm
   vii 135% of 135 km   viii 7% of 95 m

N3 HW3 Percentage increase and decrease

1 a Find these quantities without using a calculator.

   i   Increase £40 by 10% **ii** Decrease 160 m by 20%
   iii Decrease £86 by 15% **iv** Increase 740 kg by 35%
   v   Increase £48 by 17.5% **vi** Decrease 480p by 1%

b Calculate these quantities giving your answers correct to 2 decimal places.

   i   Increase £97 by 12% **ii** Decrease $78 by 27%
   iii Decrease 89 kg by 58% **iv** Increase 270 g by 86%
   v   Increase $890 by 17% **vi** Decrease 1350 m by 83%

2 Use an appropriate method to work out each of these problems. Give your answer to 2 decimal places where necessary.

   a A holiday cost £495 but it is reduced by 15% in a sale. Calculate the new price of the holiday.
   b Mr Holmes earns £456 a week. He has a pay increase of 3%. Work out how much he will earn after the pay increase.
   c A plumber charges Teresa £4389 for new central heating. If the bill is paid within 7 days he reduces the bill by 5%. Teresa pays within 7 days. Work out how much she saves.

3 Copy and complete the table.

Item	Cost price	% increase or decrease	Selling price
TV	£499	17.5% increase	
Microwave	£89.50	10% decrease	
Cooker	£245.50	20% increase	
Fridge	£389	2.5% decrease	

4 a A shop buys cakes for 50p each and sells them for 89p. What is the percentage profit?

b Paul buys a car for £3995 and sells it one year later for £3125. Work out the percentage loss.

N3 HW4 Chapter review

1 a Here are two fractions, $\frac{3}{4}$ and $\frac{2}{3}$.
   Explain which is the larger fraction.
   You may use the these grids to help your explanation.

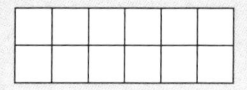

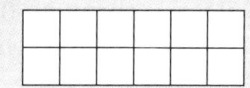

b Write these five fractions in order of size.
   Start with the smallest fraction.
   $\frac{3}{4}$ $\frac{2}{3}$ $\frac{1}{2}$ $\frac{5}{8}$ $\frac{5}{6}$

2 A 500 ml smoothie drink is made up of these juices
   33% strawberry   21% banana   22% orange
   11% grape   13% apple
   Calculate the number of ml of each type of juice.

3 Calculate these using a suitable method. Where appropriate round your answers to 2 decimal places.

   a 45% of £39
   b 17.5% of 94 m
   c 75% of $450
   d $\frac{8}{27}$ of 380 tonnes
   e $\frac{9}{16}$ of 85 kg
   f 9% of 434 mm
   g $\frac{3}{4}$ of 660 km
   h 17% of 95 m
   i 56.5% of £399
   j Increase £219 by 14%
   k Decrease $58 by $\frac{2}{3}$
   l Increase 19 kg by 13.5%
   m Decrease £999 by 22%
   n Increase £699 by 17.5%

4 Put these numbers in order of size starting with the smallest.
   a $\frac{1}{3}$, $\frac{3}{5}$, 35%, 0.3, 0.29
   b $\frac{2}{3}$, 60%, 0.62, $\frac{3}{7}$, 0.6
   c 0.12, 24%, $\frac{1}{24}$, $\frac{1}{12}$, 0.24

D3 HW1 Check-in review

1. A coin and dice are thrown together.
   Calculate the probability of getting

   a a Head and an even number **b** a Head and not a 6.
   c If the coin and dice are thrown 60 times, how many times do you expect to get a Tail and a number less than 3?

2. Claire uses a questionnaire to find out what people think about sport.
   Two questions in her questionnaire are

   What sports do you like?

   Don't you think that exercise is good for you?

   Give one criticism of each question and suggest improvements.

3. Work out:

   a $255 \div 5$ **b** $138 \div 3$ **c** $240 \div 6$
   d $174 \div 3$ **e** $693 \div 9$ **f** $520 \div 8$

4. Work out:

   a $1.5 + 3.6$ **b** $4.7 + 9.8$
   c $36.2 - 18.4$ **d** $19.4 - 3.6$

D3 HW2 Diagrams and charts

1. 60 people were asked to name their favourite colour.

   The results are shown in the table.

   Draw a bar chart to represent this information.

Colour	Frequency
Red	15
Blue	12
Green	18
Purple	5
Black	2
Other	8

2. 180 people were asked what was their favourite sport. The results were

Sport	Frequency
Football	64
Cricket	31
Rugby	28
Golf	29
Tennis	15
Other	?

   a Calculate the number of people who liked other sports.
   b Calculate the angle one person represents in a pie chart.
   c Calculate the angle of each category in the pie chart.
   d Draw the pie chart.

3. The heights, in cm, of plants in a garden were recorded.
   Draw a histogram to show the heights of the plants.

Height, h, cm	Frequency
$5 < h \leq 10$	6
$10 < h \leq 15$	13
$15 < h \leq 20$	16
$20 < h \leq 25$	9
$25 < h \leq 30$	4

4. The time taken by 120 runners in the Lake Vryney half marathon were recorded.

   Draw a frequency polygon to illustrate this information.

Time, t, hours	Frequency
$1 < t \leq 1.25$	14
$1.25 < t \leq 1.5$	26
$1.5 < t \leq 1.75$	35
$1.75 < t \leq 2$	24
$2 < t \leq 2.25$	18
$2.25 < t \leq 2.5$	3

D3 HW3 Stem-and-leaf diagrams and line graphs

1 The resting pulse rates, in beats per minute (bpm), of 30 athletes are

56 74 63 72 83 49 58 59 79 48
73 77 89 57 64 61 69 75 76 81
70 72 84 52 44 57 74 75 81 77

Draw an ordered stem-and-leaf diagram to represent this information. Choose suitable stems.

2 The heights of students in a class, in metres, to the nearest cm, are

1.60 1.45 1.51 1.63 1.70 1.46 1.38 1.44
1.52 1.39 1.50 1.48 1.60 1.52 1.36 1.70
1.63 1.55 1.49 1.36 1.45 1.42 1.51 1.67

Draw an ordered stem-and-leaf diagram to represent this information. Choose suitable stems.

3 Stephen is on a diet and his weight in kg is recorded over 10 months. His weight each month is shown.

Month	Jan	Feb	Mar	Apr	May	Jun	Jul	Aug	Sept	Oct
Weight in kg	108	103	101	99	97	94	93	95	94	94

Draw a line graph to show his weight.

4 The exam pass rate of the percentage of students gaining 5 A*–C GCSE grades for a school over 9 years is shown.

Year	1997	1998	1999	2000	2001	2002	2003	2004	2005
% 5 A*–C	37	39	41	50	54	56	60	62	59

Draw a line graph to show the percentages of 5 A*–C GCSE grades.

D3 HW4 Chapter review

1 10 men took part in a long jump competition. The table shows the heights of the 10 men and the best jumps they made.

Height of men (m)	1.70	1.80	1.65	1.75	1.65	1.74	1.60	1.75	1.60	1.67
Best jump (m)	5.33	6.00	5.00	5.95	4.80	5.72	4.60	5.80	4.40	5.04

a Plot the points on a scatter diagram.
b Describe in words the relationship between the height of the men and the maximum distance they jumped.
c State the type of correlation shown in this graph.

2 The table shows the number of units of electricity used in heating a house on ten different days and the average temperature for each day.

Average Temperature (°C)	6	2	0	6	3	5	10	8	9	12
Units of electricity used	28	38	41	34	31	31	22	25	23	22

a Plot the points on a scatter diagram.
b Describe in words the relationship between the average temperature and the number of units of electricity used.
c State the type of correlation shown in this graph.

3 In a town, 1800 cars were stolen in a year. The table below shows the times of the day when they were stolen.

Time	Number of cars
Midnight to 6 am	700
6 am to midday	80
Midday to 6 pm	280
6 pm to midnight	470
Time unknown	270

Draw a pie chart to show this information.

N4 HW1 Check-in review

1 Copy and complete the addition square, using a mental method for each calculation.

+	3.4	4.5	2.6	?	4.9	8.5
2.8				7.6		
?						13.2
3.6						
?		11.6				
9.6						
7.1						

2 Use a mental method for each of these calculations. Write the method you have used.
  a Increase 35 by 17.
  b Decrease 98 by 45.
  c What do you need to add to 745 to get 975?
  d How many more than 1398 is 2475?

3 The pie chart shows the favourite film types of 144 students.

  Calculate
  a the size of the angle for Thriller
  b the angle for Comedy
  c the angle measure that represents one student
  d the number of students who like
      i Thriller   **ii** Comedy
      iii Romance   **iv** Sci-fi

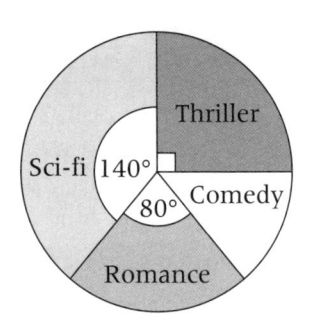

N4 HW2 Ratio

1 Write these ratios in the form $1 : n$.

a 3 : 9	b 4 : 16	c 5 : 10
d 7 : 21	e 10 : 25	f 15 : 60
g 4 : 28	h 6 : 54	i 22 : 33
j 18 : 24	k 27 : 45	l 36 : 48

2 Work out each of these problems.

 a In a school the ratio of students to staff is 45 : 2. If there are 405 students, how many staff are there?
 b In a box of chocolates the ratio of milk chocolate to plain chocolate is 5 : 4. If there are 16 plain chocolates, how many milk chocolates are there?
 c A scale on a map is 1 : 250. If the distance on the map is 7 cm, what is the distance in real life?
 d A model car has a scale of 1 : 20. What is the length of the model car if the real life car measures 4 metres?

3 Work out each of these problems.

 a Divide £30 in the ratio 1 : 4
 b Divide £120 in the ratio 5 : 7
 c Divide 84 kg in the ratio 2 : 5
 d Divide 135p in the ratio 8 : 7
 e Divide 105p in the ratio 5 : 2

4 a A plank of wood 3.2 m long is divided into three pieces in the ratio 2 : 9 : 5. How long is each piece of wood?

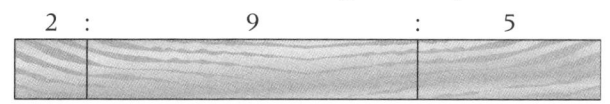

   2 :   9   :   5

 b The angles in a quadrilateral are in the ratio 1 : 2 : 4 : 5. Calculate the size of the four angles.
 c The ratio of membership of men and women at a golf club is 7 : 3. If there are 660 members at the club, how many of them are women?
 d Pete and Jo share £279.50 in the ratio 7 : 3. How much does Pete receive?

N4 HW3 Proportion and the unitary method

1 a Michelle took three tests. In Maths she scored 63 out of 72, in Science she scored 44 out of 60 and in RE she scored 29 out of 50.
   i In which subject did she do best?
   ii In which subject did she do worst?

b Leah took three different tests. In English she scored 58 out of 80, in Geography she scored 57 out of 72 and in PE she scored 51 out of 60.
   i In which subject did she do best?
   ii In which subject did she do worst?

2 a Shahzad works for 5 hours and gets paid £23.25. How much would he get paid for 7 hours?
b 4 boxes of crisps cost £9.40. What is the cost of 7 boxes of crisps?
c 40 rulers cost £8.80. What is the cost of 9 rulers?
d 7 metres of material cost £13.93. What is the cost of 3 metres of material?
e It takes 5 litres of juice to fill 40 cups. How many litres of juice are needed to fill 25 cups?

3 This is a list of ingredients for making apple and blackberry crumble for 4 people.

Work out the amount of each ingredient needed to make apple and blackberry crumble for 14 people.

> Ingredients for 4 people
> 80 g plain flour
> 60 g butter
> 4 cooking apples
> 90 g soft brown sugar
> 100 g blackberries

4 A building contractor pays nine workers £1395 for one day's work. How much would he pay
   a 5 workers   **b** 10 workers   **c** 15 workers?

N4 HW4 Chapter review

1 Write these ratios in the form $1 : n$.

   a $3 : 12$ **b** $4 : 12$ **c** $5 : 20$
   d $14 : 28$ **e** $5 : 25$ **f** $15 : 45$
   g $4 : 32$ **h** $6 : 36$ **i** $24 : 48$
   j $12 : 18$ **k** $24 : 36$ **l** $32 : 48$

Hint: The ratio can be a fraction or decimal.

2 a To make mortar you mix sand and cement in the ratio $5 : 2$. How much sand should be mixed with 20 kg of cement?

   b In a school the ratio of boys to girls is $6 : 5$. If there are 1760 students in the school, how many are girls?

   c A scale on a map is $1 : 250\,000$. If a distance on the map is 5 cm, what is the distance in real life (in metres)?

   d A model car has a scale of $3 : 40$. What is the length of the model car if the real life car measures 8 metres?

3 a Use your calculator to work out the value of $\frac{3.45 \times 6.79}{3.67 + 5.97}$

   Write all of the figures shown on your calculator display.

   b Write your answer to part **a** to an appropriate degree of accuracy.

4 The cost of 16 pens is £29.60.

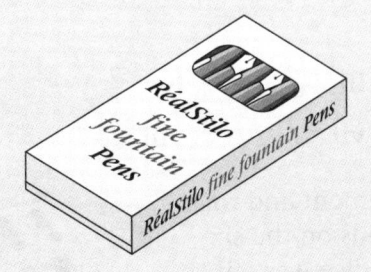

Work out the cost of 9 pens.

D4 HW1 Check-in review

1 Melissa asked 90 people what their favourite type of film was. She recorded the results in this table and used it to complete a pie chart.

Film	Frequency	Angle
Thriller	13	
Comedy	29	
Horror	5	
Science Fiction	21	
Romance	12	
Action	?	

  a Calculate the number of people who liked Action films.
  b Calculate the angle that will represent one person in the pie chart.
  c Calculate the angle for each category in the pie chart.
  d Draw the pie chart.

2 Put these in order of size starting with the smallest.
  a $\frac{3}{5}$, 65%, $\frac{7}{8}$, 0.7
  b 0.45, 49%, $\frac{4}{9}$, $\frac{4}{10}$
  c 33%, $\frac{1}{3}$, 25%, 0.3
  d 99%, 1, $\frac{9}{10}$, 0.999
  e $\frac{4}{13}$, 25%, 0.09, $\frac{1}{5}$
  f 0.15, 13%, $\frac{1}{13}$, $\frac{2}{23}$

3 Change these fractions to
  a improper fractions
    i $4\frac{3}{5}$ **ii** $6\frac{3}{7}$ **iii** $9\frac{1}{2}$ **iv** $5\frac{4}{5}$
    v $5\frac{3}{4}$ **vi** $10\frac{6}{9}$ **vii** $3\frac{2}{11}$ **viii** $12\frac{3}{5}$
  b mixed numbers
    i $\frac{6}{5}$ **ii** $\frac{9}{4}$ **iii** $\frac{12}{5}$ **iv** $\frac{7}{4}$
    v $\frac{13}{7}$ **vi** $\frac{16}{5}$ **vii** $\frac{17}{5}$ **viii** $\frac{21}{4}$

4 Claire does a statistical experiment and rolls a dice 120 times. The dice lands on the six 24 times. Would you say the dice was fair? Explain your answer.

D4 HW2 The range and averages

1 Calculate the range for each set of numbers.
  a 7, 8, 12, 4, 3
  b 1, 1, 3, 4, 4, 4, 5, 5, 5, 7, 7, 8
  c 0.45, 0.38, 0.12, 0.5, 0.75, 0.8
  d 32, 35, 33, 26, 37, 54, 23, 26
  e $1\frac{1}{2}$, 3, $4\frac{1}{4}$, 5, $3\frac{1}{4}$, 4, 5, 3, $4\frac{3}{4}$, 5
  f £3.45, £8.45, £0.45, £9.03, £4.59, £3.99

2 The heights of students in a class, in metres, are

1.60	1.45	1.51	1.63	1.70	1.46	1.38	1.44
1.52	1.39	1.50	1.48	1.60	1.52	1.36	1.70
1.63	1.55	1.49	1.36	1.45	1.42	1.51	1.67

  a Are these discrete or continuous data?
  b Calculate the range of the heights.

3 Calculate the **i** mode, **ii** median, **iii** mean of each set of numbers.
  a 1, 4, 4, 4, 4, 5, 6
  b 0, 0, 3, 2, 5, 12, 4, 4, 6
  c 3, 4, 5, 5, 4, 2, 6, 7
  d 15, 16, 12, 13, 16, 12
  e 2.4, 1.5, 2.5, 1.7, 2.8, 2.3, 1.5, 1.3

Example

Work out the missing number if the mean of these four numbers is 12.

  10   8   16 x

$10 + 8 + 16 + x = 12 \times 4 = 48$
$34 + x = 48$
$x = 14$

4 Work out the missing numbers in each set.
  a The mean of these six numbers is 10.
     5   8   14   12   9   ?
  b The mean of these five numbers is 10 and the mode is 9.
     10   9   14   ?   ?
  c The mean of these six numbers is 7, the median is 7 and the range is 9.
     10   1   8   6   ?   ?

D4 HW3 Charts and tables; comparing data

1 The number of brothers and sisters 13 students have are recorded in the table.

No. of brothers and sisters	0	1	2	3	4	5
No. of students	1	3	5	1	2	1

  a Calculate the mean, median, mode number of brothers and sisters.
  b Calculate the range in number of brothers and sisters.

2 In an English test the boys' mean score was 56% and range was 12%. The girls' mean score was 62% and range was 23%. What can you say about the performance of boys compared to girls?

3 The number of books 42 students read in one month is recorded in a pictogram.

  a What does ☐ represent?
  b Calculate the mean number of books read.
  c Calculate the proportion of students that read two or more books a month.

0	☐ ☐ ☐
1	☐ ☐ ☐ ☐
2	☐ ☐
3	☐ ☐
4	☐

4 The Key Stage 3 Maths and English results for six years are represented by these frequency polygons. Make two statements about the Maths and English KS3 test results over the 6 years.

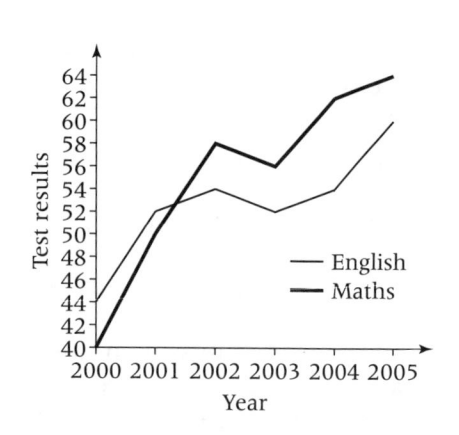

D4 HW4 Stem-and-leaf diagrams and scatter graphs

1. The heights, in m, of 18 students in a class are recorded.
   1.67 1.72 1.80 1.59 1.60 1.64 1.74 1.81 1.52
   1.56 1.73 1.83 1.89 1.76 1.65 1.69 1.76 1.77

   a Copy and complete an ordered stem-and-leaf diagram.

   15 | Key: 16 | 7 means 1.67 m
   16 |
   17 |
   18 |

   b Calculate the   i mean   ii mode   iii median   iv range.

2. The stem-and-leaf diagrams for pulse rates in beats per minute (bpm) before and after gentle exercise are

   Before exercise

   4 | 1
   5 | 1 2 2 5
   6 | 4 5 5 6 8
   7 | 0 1 1 2 2 4 6 8 8
   8 | 1 4
   9 | 0
   10 |
   11 |

   After exercise

   4 | Key: 4 | 1 means 41 bpm
   5 |
   6 | 7
   7 | 3 7 9
   8 | 2 4 8 8
   9 | 2 2 3 4 5 7 9 9
   10 | 2 4 6 7
   11 | 0 1

   a Calculate the median and range for both diagrams.
   b Make two comparisons between the pulse rate before and after exercise.

3. The table shows the heights in m, and weights in kg, of 10 footballers.

Height	1.73	1.65	1.79	1.75	1.84	1.81	1.89	1.76	1.80	1.84
Weight	73	63	82	70	83	79	91	74	84	86

   a Draw a scatter diagram to show these data on suitable axes.
   b State the type of correlation between height and weight of the football players.
   c Draw a line of best fit.
   d Use your line of best fit to estimate a footballer's
      i height if their weight is 75 kg
      ii weight if their height is 1.69 m.

D4 HW5 Chapter review

1. Some students took a mental arithmetic test. Their marks are shown in the frequency table.

Mark	Frequency
5	1
6	2
7	3
8	10
9	14
10	1

   a Work out how many students took the test.
   b Write the modal mark.

   25 students had a higher mark than Sharon.

   c Work out Sharon's mark.
   d Find the median mark.
   e Work out the range of the marks.

2. Chris asked 50 people how much they paid for a new computer.
   The results are shown in this frequency table.

Price P in £	Number of computers
$0 < P \leqslant 500$	2
$500 < P \leqslant 1000$	15
$1000 < P \leqslant 1500$	14
$1500 < P \leqslant 2000$	10
$2000 < P \leqslant 2500$	9

   Calculate an estimate for the mean price paid for a new computer.

3. The table shows the engine size and maximum speed of 10 cars.

Maximum speed (mph)	100	94	84	113	131	135	135	107	142	134
Engine size (cc)	1300	1100	1000	1600	2000	2700	2800	1400	2900	2500

   a Plot a scatter diagram for these data on suitable axes.
   b Describe the relationship between the car's engine size and its maximum speed.
   c If a car's maximum speed is 115 mph, estimate its engine size to the nearest 100.

A1 HW1 Check-in review

1. Use an approximate mental method to work out each of these problems.
   a. Sam sends 89 text messages at 9.8p a text. How much does it cost her in total?
   b. Michelle talks to her friend on the phone for 18.5 minutes. It costs 15.9p a minute. How much does the phone call cost?
   c. A shop sells these items:

Strawberries	£1.89 a box
Cherries	£2.99 a bag
Grapes	£1.87 a kg

   Work out the cost of
   i   3 boxes of strawberries
   ii 2 bags of cherries and 2 kg of grapes
   iii 1 box of strawberries, 3 bags of cherries and 3 kg of grapes.

2. A fair dice and a spinner numbered 1 – 4 are thrown together.
   a. List all the possible outcomes.
   b. If the dice and spinner were spun 240 times how many times would you expect to get a total of 10?

3. Steve is an electrician and he charges £49.50 as a call out charge and then £22.25 for each hour he works. How much does he get for 3.5 hours work?

4. Jack shares £180 between his two children Ruth and Ben. The ratio of Ruth's share to Ben's share is 5 : 4.
   a. Work out how much each child is given.

   Ben then gives 10% of his share to Ruth.

   b. Work out the percentage of the £180 that Ruth now has.

A1 HW2 Functions and linear graphs

1 For each of these functions
  i draw a function machine
  ii work out the outputs for the inputs −2, −1, 0, 1, 2, 3.
  a $4x + 2$
  b $5x - 3$
  c $\frac{1}{2}x + 4$
  d $4x - 10$

2 Match each of these function machines to a set of coordinates.

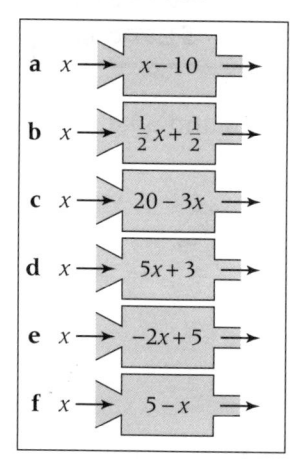

a $x \rightarrow \boxed{x - 10} \rightarrow$
b $x \rightarrow \boxed{\frac{1}{2}x + \frac{1}{2}} \rightarrow$
c $x \rightarrow \boxed{20 - 3x} \rightarrow$
d $x \rightarrow \boxed{5x + 3} \rightarrow$
e $x \rightarrow \boxed{-2x + 5} \rightarrow$
f $x \rightarrow \boxed{5 - x} \rightarrow$

A (−2, 26)(−1, 23)(0, 20)(1, 17)(2, 14)
B (−2, −7)(−1, −2)(0, 3)(1, 8)(2, 13)
C (−2, 7)(−1, 6)(0, 5)(1, 4)(2, 3)
D (−2, 9)(−1, 7)(0, 5)(1, 3)(2, 1)
E (−2, −$\frac{1}{2}$)(−1, 0)(0, $\frac{1}{2}$)(1, 1)(2, 1$\frac{1}{2}$)
F (−2, −12)(−1, −11)(0, −10)(1, −9)(2, −8)

3 a Copy and complete the table of values for $y = 4x - 2$.

x	−2	−1	0	1	2
y					

  b Write the coordinate pairs.
  c Plot the line $y = 4x - 2$ onto a grid with appropriate axes.

4 a Copy and complete the table of values for $y = -2x + 4$.

x	−2	−1	0	1	2
y					

  b Write the coordinate pairs.
  c Plot the line $y = -2x + 4$ onto a grid with appropriate axes.

A1 HW3 More linear graphs

1 On a copy of the grid, draw graphs of these functions.
  a $y = 3x + 1$
  b $y = 2x + 1$
  c $y = -3x + 1$
  d $y = -2x + 1$
  e What do you notice about the functions and their graphs?

2 a On a copy of the grid, draw the graph of $x + y = 4$.
  b Rearrange the equation to make y the subject.
  c i Use your equation to find y when x equals 3.
    ii Use your graph to check your answer.
  d Use your graph to find x when y equals 2.5.

3 Draw these graphs on the same set of axes.
  a $y = 4$ **b** $x = -2$
  c $y = 0$ **d** $x = 6$
  e Write the coordinates where
    i $y = 4$ and $x = -2$ cross
    ii $y = 0$ and $x = 6$ cross.
    iii What do you notice?
  f Without drawing the graphs of $y = 6$ and $x = -2$, what will be the coordinates where they cross?

4 a Draw the graph of $y = 2x - 1$.
  b On the same set of axes draw the graph of $y = 5$.
  c Write the coordinates of point P where the graphs cross.

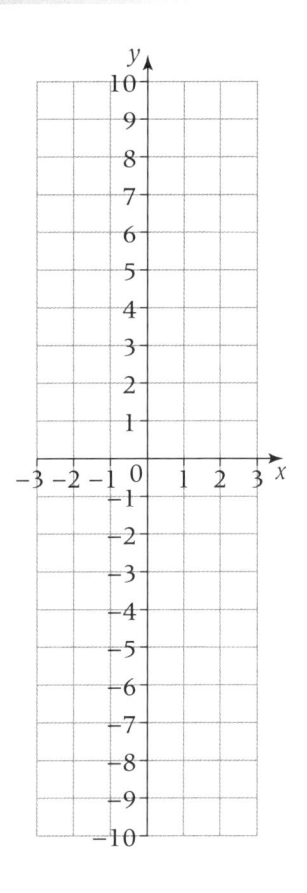

A1 HW4 Chapter review

1 Match the equations to the graphs of straight lines.

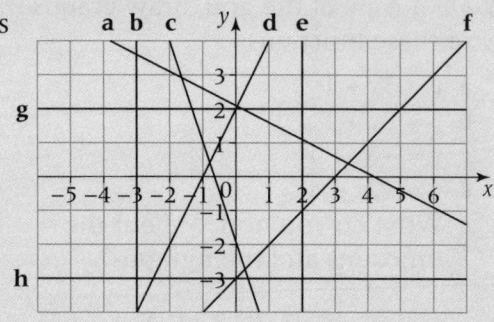

$y = -3$
$y = x - 3$
$x = -3$
$x = 2$
$y = 2$
$y = -3x - 2$
$y = 2x + 2$
$y = -\frac{1}{2}x + 2$ $y = -x - 3$

Hint: Beware, there are some extra equations!

2 ABCD is a parallelogram. A is the point (0, 3). C is the point (0, −3). The equation of the straight line through A and B is $y = \frac{1}{2}x + 3$.

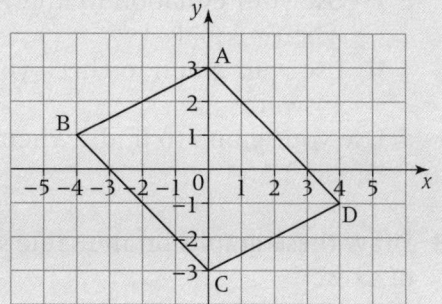

  a Find the equation of the line through C and D.
  b Find the equation of the line passing through A and D.
  c Calculate the coordinates of the midpoint of the line segment CD.

3 a Copy and complete the table of values for $y = 3x + 2$.

x	−2	−1	0	1	2	3
y		−1	2			

  b On a grid, draw the graph of $y = 3x + 2$.
  c Use your graph to find
     i the value of y when $x = -1.5$
     ii the value of x when $y = 3.5$

4 Write three equations of straight lines that are parallel to
  a $y = 4x - 5$ **b** $y = -5x - 5$

N5 HW1 Check-in review

1 If 3.46 × 457 = 1581.22
Write the answer to
  a 0.346 × 4570
  b 34.6 × 0.457

2 Copy the grid, extend the axes to +10, and draw these straight line graphs.
  a $y = 4x + 4$
  b $y = 2x - 3$
  c $y = 3x$
  d $y = -2x + 1$

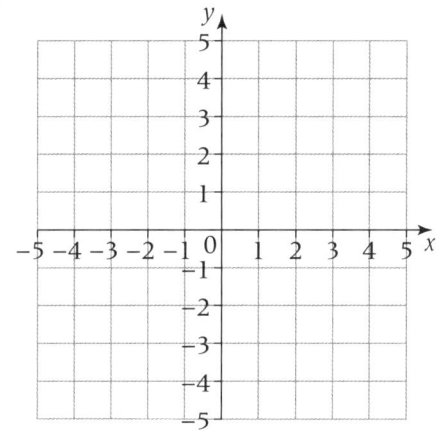

3 Use an appropriate method to calculate these amounts. Write the method you have used.
  a 67 × 100
  b 56 × 5
  c 69 × 8
  d 2388 ÷ 6
  e 312 ÷ 8
  f 16.3 × 24
  g 56.6 × 30
  h 273 ÷ 7
  i 32.5 × 6
  j 5.29 × 6.5
  k 77 × 5.8
  l 16 × 0.5

N5 HW2 Squares, cubes and roots

1. Use your calculator, where necessary, to work out these powers and roots.

   a 6^2 b 14^2 c 4^3
   d 1^3 e 15^2 f $(-6)^2$
   g 7^3 h 12^3 i 10^3
   j $\sqrt{81}$ k $\sqrt{169}$ l $\sqrt[3]{64}$
   m $\sqrt[3]{17\,576}$ n $\sqrt{4900}$ o $\sqrt[3]{1000}$

2. Use the trial and improvement method to find the square root of each of these numbers to 1 decimal place. Record your results in a table. The first one has been started for you.

   a $\sqrt{90}$

Estimate	Check (square of estimate)	Answer	Too big or too small
9	9^2	81	Too small
10	10^2	100	Too big
9.5	9.5^2	90.5	Too big

   b $\sqrt{70}$ c $\sqrt{120}$ d $\sqrt{250}$

3. Some numbers can be represented as the sum of two squares.
   For example, $4^2 + 5^2 = 16 + 25 = 41$

   Find all the numbers between 1 and 50 that can be represented as the sum of two square numbers.

4. Use the trial and improvement method to find the cube root of each of these numbers to 2 decimal places. Record your results in a table.

   a $\sqrt[3]{10}$ b $\sqrt[3]{60}$ c $\sqrt[3]{135}$ d $\sqrt[3]{400}$

N5 HW3 Factors and powers

1 Use the x^y-button (or power key) on your calculator to work out these questions. In each case, copy the question and find the value of x.

  a $4^x = 16$
  b $5^x = 125$
  c $10^x = 1\,000\,000$
  d $x^4 = 4096$
  e $2^x = 1024$
  f $x^{10} = 1$
  g $3^x = 531\,441$
  h $x^9 = 10\,077\,696$
  i $19^x = 1$

2 Simplify each of these, leaving your answer as a single power of a number.

  a $2^3 \times 2^4$
  b $5^6 \times 5^3$
  c $3^{12} \div 3^4$
  d $6^3 \div 6^2$
  e $a^3 \times a^6$
  f $b^4 \div b$
  g $\dfrac{4^5 \times 4^9}{4^4}$
  h $\dfrac{5^4 \times 5^{10} \times 5}{5^6}$
  i $\dfrac{p^4 \times p^4}{p^3}$
  j $\dfrac{w^4 \times w}{w}$
  k $\dfrac{s \times s^3}{s^2}$
  l $\dfrac{f^5 \times f}{f^5}$

3 Write down the numbers inside the oval that are

  a odd numbers
  b square numbers
  c cube numbers
  d factors of 18
  e prime factors of 36
  f highest common factor of 24 and 18
  g lowest common multiple of 6 and 4.

  Numbers in oval: 2, 24, 144, 3, 6, 24, 1, 36, 49, 16, 8, 4, 216, 100, 5, 9, 1000

4 Work out the value of each of these expressions.

  a $3^2 \times 4$
  b $2^4 \times 5^2$
  c $3 \times 5^3 \times 11$
  d $3^2 \times 5 \times 13$
  e $2 \times 5^3 \times 3$
  f $2 \times 11^2 \times 13$
  g 3×11^4
  h $5^3 \times 11^2$
  i $2 \times 3 \times 5 \times 13$

5 a Express 72 as a product of its prime factors.
  b Find the highest common factor (HCF) of 72 and 24.

N5 HW4　Chapter review

1 Here are some numbers.

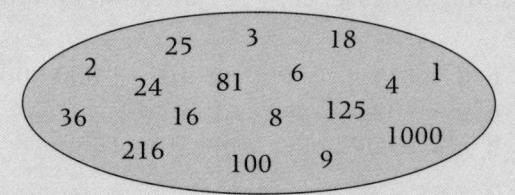

> 2, 25, 3, 18, 24, 81, 6, 4, 1, 36, 16, 8, 125, 1000, 216, 100, 9

From the numbers inside the oval, write the numbers that are

  a prime numbers
  b square numbers
  c cube numbers
  d factors of 24
  e prime factors of 18
  f factors of both 24 and 36.
  g Salma says '6 is a cube number because $2^3 = 6$.'
  Salma is wrong. Explain why.

2 Work out the value of

  a $(3^2)^3$
  b $(\sqrt{4})^2$
  c $a^2 \times a^4$
  d $\dfrac{3^4 \times 3^5}{3}$
  e 5^0

3 a Find the highest common factor (HCF) of 108 and 36
  b Find the highest common factor (HCF) of 72 and 96.

4 1800 can be expressed by the products of prime factors
  $2^x \times 3^y \times 5^z$
  Find the values of x, y and z.

A2 HW1 Check-in review

1 Use the information that

$17 \times 16 = 272$

To find the least common multiple (LCM) of 17 and 32.

2 a Copy and complete this table for the function $y = 2x + 4$.

x	0	1	2	3	4	5
y						

  b On a copy of the grid, draw the graph of $y = 2x + 4$.
  c Draw the lines $y = 9$ and $x = 3$ on the same grid.
  d Write the equation of a line that is parallel to $y = 2x + 4$.

3 Calculate the coordinates of the midpoint between the points

  a (2, 2) and (6, 4)
  b (3, 0) and (9, 0)
  c (−2, 2) and (6, −4)

4 Round these numbers to the given degree of accuracy.

  a 46.456   (1 decimal place)
  b 67.945   (2 decimal places)
  c 356.4589   (3 decimal places)
  d 13.96   (1 decimal place)
  e 34.5683   (2 decimal places)
  f 13.998   (2 decimal places)

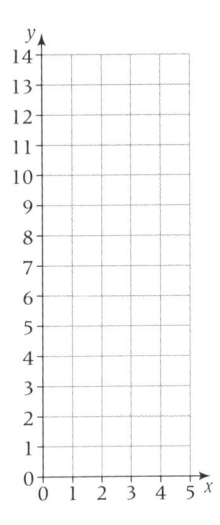

A2 HW2 Algebraic expressions and indices

1 Simplify these expressions.

a $3a + b + 3a + 2b$
b $5d + 4e - 2d + e + d$
c $4f + 5g + 6f - 7g + f$
d $4h - i + 3h - 5i + h$
e $3j + 5k + k - 5k - k$
f $6l + 4m - 5l - 4m - l + m$

2 An ice cream van sells large ice creams and small ice creams.

The cost of the large ice cream is 90 pence and the small ice cream is 50 pence.

Ice creams
Large 90 pence
Small 50 pence

Write an expression for the cost of buying p large ice creams and s small ice creams.

Example

Simplify **a** $s^4 \times s^2$ **b** $\dfrac{n^2}{n}$

a $s^4 \times s^2 = s^{(4+2)} = s^6$ **b** $\dfrac{n^2}{n} = n^{(2-1)} = n$

---

3 Simplify these expressions.

a $y \times y \times y \times y$
b $2 \times r \times r \times r \times s \times s$
c $3 \times b \times b \times a \times a \times a$
d $a^2 \times a^4$
e $r^3 \times 3r^2$
f $b^3 \times b^2 \times b$
g $3r^2 \times 2r^3$
h $5p^3 \times 3q^2$
i $4b \times 2b^3$
j $\dfrac{p^3}{p^2}$
k $\dfrac{z^5}{z^2}$
l $\dfrac{g^3}{g}$

4 Simplify each of these expressions.

a $\dfrac{a^3 \times a^3}{a^2}$
b $\dfrac{q^5 \times q^2}{q^4}$
c $\dfrac{k \times k^3}{k^2}$
d $\dfrac{t \times t^3 \times t^2}{t^4}$
e $\dfrac{u^4 \times u^3 \times u^2}{u}$
f $\dfrac{s \times s^2 \times s^2}{s^3 \times s}$
g $\dfrac{p \times p \times p^3}{p^2}$
h $\dfrac{r^5 \times r \times r^2}{r^3}$
i $\dfrac{v^5 \times v^3 \times v}{v^4}$

A2 HW3 Expanding brackets and simplifying

Example

Expand and simplify $4(2m + 1) - 2(m + 1)$

$4(2m + 1) - 2(m + 1) = 8m + 4 - 2m - 2$
$ = 6m + 2$

1 Expand and simplify (where necessary) these expressions.

   a $3(x + 4)$ **b** $5(x - 3)$
   c $4(6 + x)$ **d** $3(x + 5) + x$
   e $4(3x - 3) + 2x$ **f** $3(3x + 2) + 3x + 2$
   g $6(3x - 3) + 2x$ **h** $5(2x + 1) - 3$
   i $2(5x + 5) + 3x - 2$ **j** $7(3x - 3) + 4 - x$

2 Expand and simplify these expressions.

   a $3(2x + 3) + 5(2x + 4)$ **b** $4(2x + 4) + 2(4x + 3)$
   c $4(3x + 2) + 3(2x + 3)$ **d** $2(3x + 5) + 4(4x + 5)$
   e $2(5x + 4) + 4(7x + 3)$ **f** $2(3x + 3) + 5(x + 3)$
   g $4(2x + 3) + 4(x - 2)$ **h** $3(2x + 3) + 6(3x + 3)$
   i $5(x + 3) + 5(4x - 3)$ **j** $7(2x - 4) + 3(3x + 1)$

3 Expand these expressions.

   a $x(3x + 2)$ **b** $x(x^2 + 3)$
   c $3x(x^2 - 3)$ **d** $3x(x + 2)$
   e $2x(x^2 - 3)$ **f** $4x^2(x^2 + 2)$
   g $5x(x^3 + 2)$ **h** $4x(x^2 + 3)$
   i $2x^2(x - 4)$ **j** $4x^2(x + 5)$

4 Expand and simplify these expressions.

   a $3(x + 3) + 3(x - 2)$ **b** $4(3x + 4) + 3(x - 3)$
   c $5(2x + 4) - 4(x + 3)$ **d** $4(3x - 2) - 4(x + 3)$
   e $3(3x + 4) - 4(2x - 3)$ **f** $5(x + 3) - 4(2x - 2)$
   g $5(2x - 3) - 4(3x - 2)$ **h** $2(2x + 4) + 3(2x - 4)$
   i $4(x + 4) - 4(x - 4)$ **j** $2(2x - 1) - 4(x - 1)$

A2 HW4 Chapter review

1 Factorise these expressions.

   a $2x + 14$ **b** $5x + 20$
   c $4x + 8$ **d** $3x - 9$
   e $6x + 8$ **f** $12x + 4$
   g $10 - 5x$ **h** $22x + 6$
   i $20 + 4x$ **j** $16x - 10$

2 Factorise these expressions.

   a $x^2 + x$ **b** $3x + x^2$
   c $3x^2 + 3$ **d** $4x^2 + 2x$
   e $3x^3 - 6x$ **f** $5x^4 + x^3$
   g $x^2 - 4x$ **h** $4x - 12x^2$
   i $5x^2 + 25x$ **j** $10x^2 - 2x$

3 a Simplify

      i $4g + 6g$
      ii $3t \times 6p$

   b Expand $6(3y - 4)$
   c Expand and simplify $3(3p + 5) - 3(5p - 6)$

4 a Factorise $x^2 - 4x$
   b Simplify $d^5 \div d^3$
   c Expand and simplify

      i $5(x + 4) + 4(x - 6)$
      ii $3x^2(x + 4) + 3(x^3 - 2)$

5 These cards show expansions and factorisations.
   Match the cards in pairs and write out each pair.

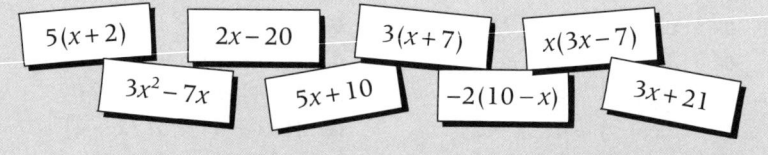

   | $5(x + 2)$ | $2x - 20$ | $3(x + 7)$ | $x(3x - 7)$ |

   | $3x^2 - 7x$ | $5x + 10$ | $-2(10 - x)$ | $3x + 21$ |

A3 HW1 Check-in review

1 Here are the equations of five straight lines.
They are labelled from A to E.
Copy the table and put a tick to show the lines that are parallel.

A	$2y-x=6$	
B	$y-3x=5$	
C	$2y=6x+12$	
D	$y+1=3x$	
E	$6x+1=2y$	

2 Write the equations of these lines in order of steepness, starting with the least steep.

   a $y = 4x + 2$ **b** $3x - y = 10$
   c $y = \frac{1}{2}x + 5$ **d** $6y - 2x = 12$
   e $3y - x = 20$ **f** $y = \frac{3}{4}x - 4$
   g $y - 8x = 5$ **h** $15x - 10y = 20$

3 Expand and simplify these expressions.

   a $3(x + 4)$ **b** $4x(x + 5)$
   c $2x(x - 5)$ **d** $x^2(x + 4x)$

4 Write each of these ratios in the form $1 : n$.

   a $3 : 12$ **b** $5 : 35$ **c** $16 : 480$
   d $65p : £4.55$ **e** $35\,g : 35\,kg$ **f** $0.18 : 5.76$

5 Simplify these expressions.

   a $4x + y + 3x$ **b** $8x - y + 2y$
   c $x - 3y + 2x$ **d** $x - 4y + 6z - 5x - 6x + y$
   e $6x + y - 4x - y + 2x$ **f** $9x - 4y + 2x - 6y$
   g $x + y - x - y$ **h** $9x + 6y - z - 4y + 2z$

A3 HW2   Harder linear graphs

1 Draw the graphs of these functions, each on a separate grid with axes from +10 to −10.

a $y = 2x + 4$
b $y = 5x - 4$
c $x + y = 5$
d $4x - y = 5$

2 a Draw the graphs of these functions on the same grid with axes from +10 to −10.

i $y = 3x + 1$
ii $y = 3x - 1$
iii $y = 3x$
iv $y = 3x + 4$

What do you notice?

b Draw the graphs of these functions on the same grid with axes from +10 to −10.

i $y = -2x + 4$
ii $y = -2x$
iii $y = -2x + 5$
iv $y = -2x - 4$

What do you notice?

3 a Rearrange these equations into the form $y = mx + c$.

i $2x + y = 6$
ii $3y - 6x = -9$
iii $10y + 5x = 40$
iv $2y - 4x = -10$

b Write the equation of the line parallel to line $y = 2x + 6$.

4 Write the equations of these lines in order of steepness, starting with the least steep.

a $y = 3x + 4$
b $2x - y = 10$
c $y = 4x + 5$
d $6y - 3x = 12$
e $4y + x = 20$
f $y = \frac{3}{4}x - 2$
g $y - 10x = 5$
h $5x - 4y = 20$

A3 HW3 Conversion graphs

1 Use the conversion graph to convert

  a 10 lb to kg
  b 6 kg to lb
  c 20 lb to kg
  d 18 kg to lb
  e 8.8 lb to kg
  f Put these weights into order starting with the lightest
  10 lb, 7 kg, 10 kg, 3 lb, 8 kg, 4.4 lb, 9 kg

Conversion graph for pounds to kilograms

2 Find out the current exchange rate for pounds to euros.
On graph paper draw a conversion graph with pounds on the y-axis going up to £200.
Use your conversion graph to convert

  a £100 into euros
  b £60 into euros
  c £130 into euros
  d €160 into pounds
  e €80 into pounds
  f €300 into pounds

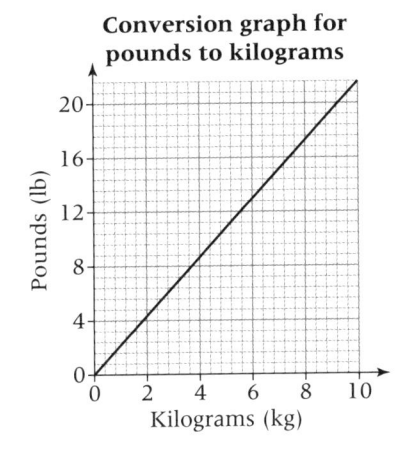

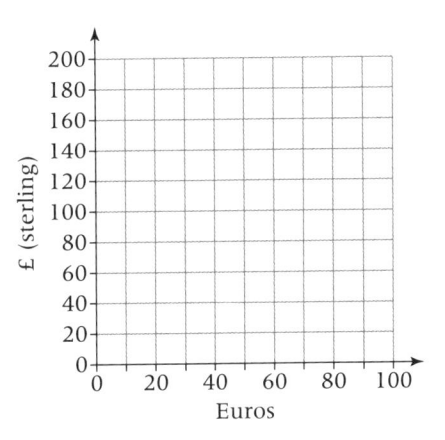

3 a Draw a conversion graph to convert between pints and litres using
  1 litre = $1\frac{3}{4}$ pints, 5 pints = $8\frac{3}{4}$ litres and 10 pints = $17\frac{1}{2}$ litres.

  b Use the conversion graph to convert

   i 6 pints to litres
   ii 10 litres to pints
   iii 15 pints to litres
   iv 20 litres to pints

A3 HW4 Distance–time graphs and speed

1 Anna goes for a run to the park. This distance–time graph illustrates her journey.

  a How long does it take her to reach the park?
  b How long does she stay at the park?
  c When was she running the slowest?
  d How far did she run in total?

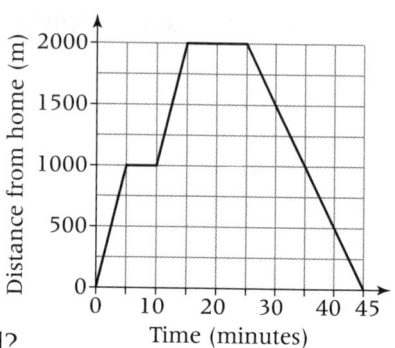

2 The distance–time graph illustrates a journey.

  a What happened at 10.30 am?
  b How long did they stop when they were 65 miles from home?
  c Using the conversion of 80 miles = 128 kilometres convert the total distance covered in miles to km.

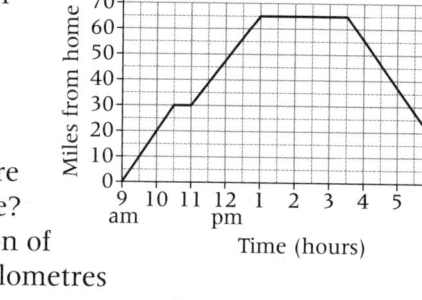

3 The graph shows Teresa's journey to the shops.

  a How many times did she stop on the way?
  b Using the formula
  $$\text{speed} = \frac{\text{distance}}{\text{time}}$$
  work out the speed in metres per minute between
   i 0 and 10 minutes
   ii 20 and 60 minutes
   iii 85 and 100 minutes.

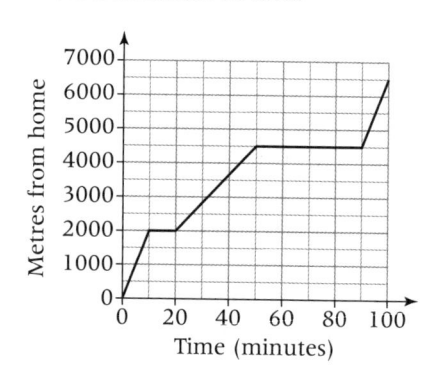

A3 HW5 Chapter review

1 Here is part of a travel graph of David's journey from his house to the shops and back.

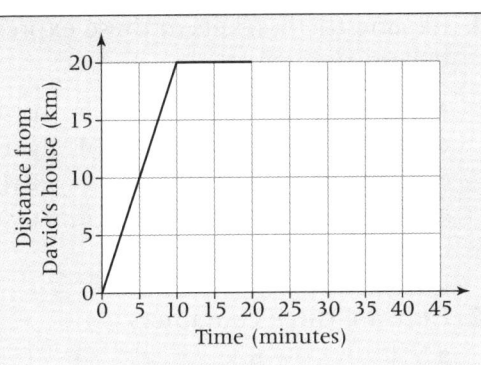

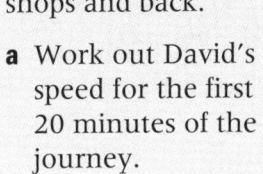

  a Work out David's speed for the first 20 minutes of the journey.

David spent 10 minutes at the shops.
He then travelled back to his house at 80 km/h.

  b Copy and complete the travel graph.

Hint: If Speed = $\frac{Distance}{Time}$, Distance = Speed × Time, and Time = $\frac{Distance}{Speed}$.

2 The temperature y °F is approximately related to the temperature x °C by the formula
$$30 = y - 2x$$
  a Rearrange this formula into the form $y = mx + c$.
  b Draw a graph of this formula on a grid from −20 to 40. Use your graph to find
  ci y when $x = 15$ °C
  cii y when $x = -10$ °C
  ciii x when $y = 0$ °F
  civ x when $y = 100$ °F

3 Sketch a graph to show the depth of water against time when these containers are filled.

  a **b**  **c** 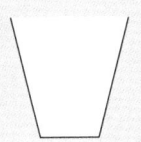 **d**

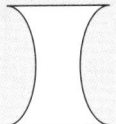

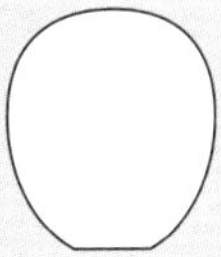

A4 HW1 Check-in review

1 Expand the brackets in these expressions and simplify where necessary.

  a $3(x+5)$ **b** $4(x-4)$
  c $x(x+4)$ **d** $2(2x+5)$
  e $-3(x+3)$ **f** $-2x(x+4)$
  g $3(x+4)+4(x-4)$ **h** $3(x-4)+6(x-2)$
  i $5(x-2)+7(x+3)$

2 Here are three containers.

  a   **b**   **c**

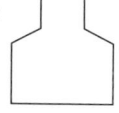

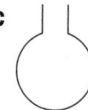

Water is poured into each container at a steady rate. Match the correct graph of water height against time to its container.

  i   **ii** 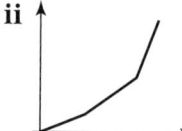   **iii**

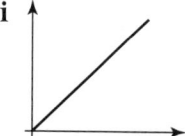

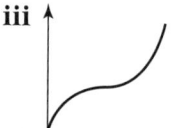

3 **a** List all the factors of 36.
    b List all the factors of 48.
    c Find the highest common factor of 36 and 48.

4 Simplify each quantity, leaving your answer as a single power.

  a $5^2 \times 5^3$
  b $7^6 \div 7^4$
  c $10^4 \times 10^4$
  d $x^9 \div x^5$

A4 HW2 Term-to-term rules; the general term

1 Write out the first five terms of these sequences.

  a 1st term 4, increases by 5 each time
  b 3rd term 5, decreases by 3 each time
  c 2nd term 8, increases by 2 each time
  d 3rd term −1, increases by 4 each time
  e 2nd term 0, decreases by 3 each time
  f 5th term 6, increases by 3 each time

2 For each of these sequences

  i work out the three missing terms
  ii describe the sequence.

  a 4, 7, __, 13, 16, __, 22, __
  b 20, __, 12, 8, 4, __, __
  c 7, 5, __, 1, __, __
  d __, 10, 8, __, __, 2
  e __, −15, −11, __, __, 1
  f __, 15, __, 3, __

3 Find the first 3 terms and the 10th term of the sequences with nth term

  a $4n + 4$
  b $5n + 2$
  c $6n - 4$
  d $3n + 5$
  e $10n + 3$
  f $10 - 2n$

4 Find the first 5 terms of the sequences with nth term

  a $n^2 + 3$
  b $n^2 - 3$
  c $2n^2 + 3$
  d $3n^2 - 4$
  e $10 - n^2$
  f $4n^2 - 5$

A4 HW3 Finding the *n*th term; pattern sequences

1 Copy and complete these tables for linear sequences.

a
Pattern number	1	2	3	4	5	n
Term	4	10		22	28	

b
Pattern number	1	2	3	4	5	n
Term	15	18		24		

c
Pattern number	1	2	3	4	5	n
Term		−5	−3		1	

2 Find the *n*th term for these sequences.

  a 12, 14, 16, 18, 20, …
  b 7, 12, 17, 22, 27, …
  c 10, 19, 28, 37, 46, …
  d 25, 22, 19, 16, 13, 10, …
  e −3, −1, 1, 3, 5, 7, …
  f −6, −9, −12, −15, −18, −21, …

3 Here is a sequence.

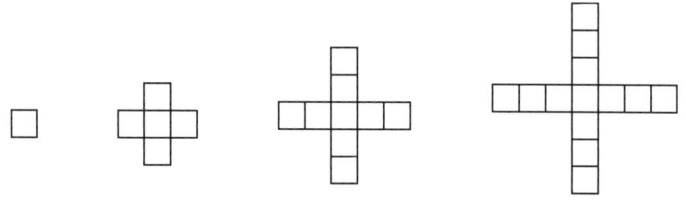

  a Write the number of squares in the next two patterns.
  b Find, in terms of n, an expression for the number of squares in the *n*th pattern.
  c Find the number of squares in the 50th pattern.

4 Repeat question **3** for this sequence of dots.

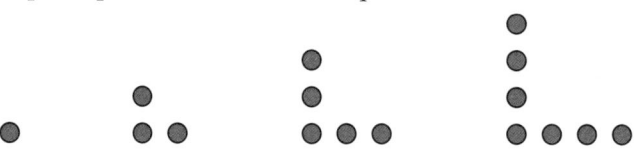

A4 HW4 Chapter review

1 Here is a pattern made from matchsticks.

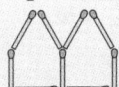

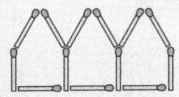

a Draw the next pattern in the sequence.
b Copy and complete the table.

Pattern number	1	2	3	4	5	n
Term						

c Use the general formula to work out how many matchsticks are needed for the 10th pattern.

2 Here is a pattern of hexagons.

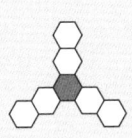

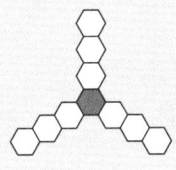

a Copy and complete the table.

Pattern number	1	2	3	4	5	n
Term						

b Use the general formula to work out how many hexagons are needed for the 50th pattern.

3 Here is a pattern of triangles.

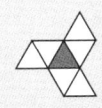

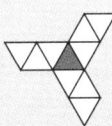

Work out, using the general formula, how many triangles there will be in the 20th pattern.

4 Find the nth term for this sequence
10, 14, 18, 22, 26, 30, ...

N6 HW1 Check-in review

1 Simplify each fraction.

    a $\dfrac{2}{4}$ **b** $\dfrac{9}{12}$ **c** $\dfrac{20}{25}$ **d** $\dfrac{9}{27}$

    e $\dfrac{40}{32}$ **f** $\dfrac{54}{60}$ **g** $\dfrac{70}{110}$ **h** $\dfrac{45}{50}$

2 Write the first terms for the sequence with nth term

    a $3n + 1$ **b** $5n + 3$ **c** $n^2 + 5$

    d $4n - 2$ **e** $9 - 3n$ **f** $2n^2 - 4$

3 Copy each of these calculations and insert brackets, where necessary, to make each statement correct. Not every statement needs brackets!

    a $3 + 5 \times 2 = 16$
    b $8 \div 2 - 2 = 2$
    c $7 \times 3 + 9 \div 4 = 21$
    d $52 - 5 \times 2 + 6 = 21$
    e $6 \times 32 - 5 = 24$
    f $4 + 6 \times 9 = 58$
    g $5 + 40 \div 8 = 10$
    h $33 + 6 \times 5 = 165$

4 Simplify

    a $4p^2 \times 3$

    b $4r^2 \times 2s^3$

    c $4m^3 \times 2m$

    d $\dfrac{y^2 \times y^3 \times y^4}{y \times y^5}$

N6 HW2 Fraction calculations

1 Calculate each of these, giving your answer in its simplest form where appropriate.

a $\frac{1}{4} + \frac{1}{4}$
b $\frac{2}{9} + \frac{4}{9}$
c $\frac{10}{19} - \frac{4}{19}$
d $\frac{4}{15} + \frac{6}{15}$
e $\frac{23}{28} - \frac{2}{28}$
f $\frac{4}{25} + \frac{14}{25}$
g $\frac{17}{11} - \frac{6}{11}$
h $\frac{12}{7} + \frac{14}{7}$
i $\frac{17}{13} - 1$

2 Calculate each of these, giving your answer in its simplest form where appropriate.

a $\frac{1}{3} + \frac{1}{6}$
b $\frac{4}{5} - \frac{3}{10}$
c $\frac{1}{3} - \frac{1}{4}$
b $\frac{3}{7} + \frac{6}{21}$
e $\frac{4}{5} + \frac{3}{4}$
f $\frac{4}{9} + \frac{3}{4}$
g $\frac{7}{12} - \frac{1}{7}$
h $\frac{4}{5} - \frac{1}{8}$
i $\frac{8}{9} + \frac{4}{5}$

Hint: Write both fractions as equivalent fractions with the same denominator.

3 Calculate each of these, leaving your answer in its simplest form.

a $3 \times \frac{2}{5}$
b $\frac{4}{5} \times 2$
c $\frac{4}{11} \times 3$
d $\frac{2}{7} \times \frac{7}{10}$
e $\frac{5}{8} \times \frac{5}{6}$
f $\frac{3}{11} \times \frac{1}{3}$
g $7 \times \frac{8}{9}$
h $\frac{5}{7} \times \frac{2}{3}$
i $\frac{9}{11} \times \frac{3}{5}$
j $3\frac{3}{4} \times 4$
k $1\frac{2}{3} \times 9$
l $1\frac{1}{2} \times 2\frac{3}{4}$

4 Calculate each of these, leaving your answer in its simplest form.

a $5 \div \frac{7}{8}$
b $8 \div \frac{1}{9}$
c $9 \div \frac{3}{4}$
d $\frac{2}{5} \div 4$
e $\frac{3}{7} \div 3$
f $\frac{4}{13} \div \frac{3}{5}$
g $\frac{4}{7} \div \frac{1}{3}$
h $\frac{9}{11} \div \frac{3}{7}$
i $\frac{1}{2} \div \frac{6}{7}$
j $3\frac{3}{4} \div \frac{1}{3}$
k $\frac{8}{9} \div 1\frac{2}{3}$
l $3\frac{4}{5} \div 5\frac{1}{4}$

5 For each pair of fractions choose either < or > to show which fraction is greater.

a $\frac{1}{4}$ and $\frac{1}{5}$
b $\frac{9}{10}$ and $\frac{9}{12}$
c $\frac{7}{10}$ and $\frac{4}{5}$
d $\frac{4}{5}$ and $\frac{19}{25}$
e $\frac{5}{12}$ and $\frac{1}{4}$
f $\frac{29}{100}$ and $\frac{3}{10}$

N6 HW3 Decimal calculations

1 Work out:
   a 1.5 + 3.6
   b 4.7 + 9.8
   c 36.2 − 18.4
   d 19.4 − 3.6

2 Calculate these, giving your answer to the stated number of decimal places:
   a 2.4 × 13.7 (1 d.p.)
   b 97.6 × 3.5 (2 d.p.)
   c 15.4 ÷ 3.6 (2 d.p.)
   d 48.3 ÷ 11.2 (2 d.p.)

3 Use the information given to work out each of these calculations without using a calculator.
   a 37 × 43 = 1591   What is 37 × 4.3?
   b 87 × 69 = 6003   What is 8.7 × 6.9?
   c 64 × 61 = 3904   What is 6.4 × 61?
   d 58 × 83 = 4814   What is 0.58 × 83?
   e 39 × 59 = 2301   What is 3900 × 59?

4 3.56 × 840 = 2990.4
   Write the answer to
   a 0.356 × 8400
   b 2990.4 ÷ 35.6
   c 35.6 × 0.84

5 Sanjay mends computers.
   He charges
      £46.80 for the first hour on a computer and
      £32.50 for each extra hour's work.
   Sanjay repaired a computer and charged a total of £241.80.
   Without using a calculator and showing all of your workings, work out how many hours it took Sanjay to mend the computer.

N6 HW4 Chapter review

1. Calculate these and give your answer in its simplest form.

   a $\frac{1}{4} + \frac{1}{8}$ b $\frac{3}{5} - \frac{3}{10}$ c $\frac{1}{3} - \frac{1}{6}$

   d $\frac{2}{7} + \frac{3}{14}$ e $\frac{1}{5} + \frac{7}{10}$ f $\frac{4}{9} + \frac{1}{3}$

   g $\frac{7}{4} - \frac{1}{5}$ h $\frac{4}{7} - \frac{1}{3}$ i $\frac{1}{7} + \frac{4}{5}$

   Hint: Write both fractions as equivalent fractions with the same denominator.

2. Calculate these, leaving your answers as fractions in their simplest form where necessary.

   a What is the total weight of 9 shopping bags each weighing 2.5 kg?
   b Elaine takes $\frac{3}{5}$ of an hour to run 5 miles. How long does it take her to run 12.5 miles?
   c A rectangle is $\frac{2}{5}$ m long and $\frac{4}{7}$ m wide. What is the area of the rectangle? What is the perimeter of the rectangle?

3. Calculate these, using an appropriate method

   a 25% of 600
   b 80% of 560
   c 15% of £4.80
   d 7% of £630

4. Gary buys 7.6 kg of potatoes. Each kilogram of potatoes costs £0.90. How much money does Gary pay for the potatoes?

A5 HW1 Check-in review

1 a Expand $\quad x(4x^2 + 3)$
  b Simplify $\quad 3x^3y \times 4x^2y^2$
  c Factorise $\quad 5x^3 + 12x$

2 Using this formula work out the volume of each shape.
   Volume of a prism = Area of cross-section × length

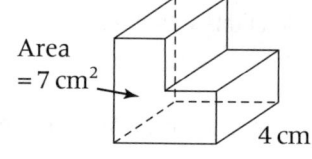

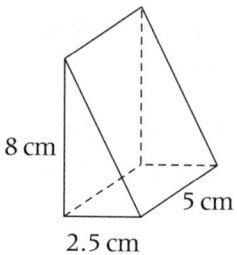

   a Area = 7 cm², 4 cm

   b 8 cm, 5 cm, 2.5 cm

   Hint: area of triangle = $\frac{1}{2}$ × base × height

3 Write a suitable estimate for each of these calculations.
   In each case clearly show how you estimated your answer.

   a $21.5 + 23.5$
   b $578 - 215$
   c 2.98×5.05
   d $19.75 \div 3.76$
   e 49.98×4.87
   f $86.7 \div 2.85$
   g $\dfrac{5.6 \times 9.7}{3.87}$
   h $\dfrac{29.7 \times 21.3}{39.6}$
   i $\dfrac{29.55 \times 21.4^2}{6.1}$

A5 HW2 Solving equations

1 Solve these equations.

a $a + 10 = 14$
b $p + 3 = 10$
c $4f = 12$
d $\frac{p}{3} = 5$
e $4g = 20$
f $t - 4 = 23$
g $s + 5 = 24$
h $6y = 36$
i $20 - d = 13$
j $\frac{x}{5} = 9$
k $3r = 81$
l $100 - r = 54$

2 For each of these 'think of a number' problems
  i write an equation   ii solve the equation.

a I think of a number and add five. The answer is 30.
b I think of a number and subtract 4. The answer is 12.
c I think of a number and multiply it by 7. The answer is 21.
d I think of a number and divide it by 8. The answer is 4.
e I think of a number and subtract it from 15. The answer is 8.

3 Solve these equations.

a $3b + 4 = 13$
b $6f - 3 = 9$
c $4f + 2 = 22$
d $\frac{p}{3} + 3 = 7$
e $5m - 3 = 22$
f $\frac{r}{4} - 5 = 0$
g $4d + 6 = 38$
h $4r - 10 = -2$
i $6k + 4 = 19$
j $6t + 5 = -13$
k $\frac{f}{3} + 4 = 1$
l $9p - 4 = -31$

4 For each of these 'think of a number' problems
  i write an equation   ii solve the equation.

a I think of a number, multiply it by 3 then add 2. The answer is 17.
b I think of a number, divide it by 5 then add 6. The answer is 10.
c I think of a number, multiply it by 7 then subtract 8. The answer is 20.
d I think of a number, divide it by 4 then subtract 4. The answer is −8.

A5 HW3 Harder equations

1 The diagram shows a square with sides $4y + 3$.

  a Write an expression for the perimeter of the square.
  b The perimeter of the square is 108 cm. Find the value of y.

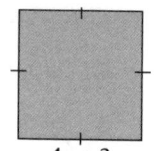

2 The diagram shows a rectangle of side lengths $2x - 3$ and 5.

  a Write an expression for the area of the rectangle.
  b The area of the rectangle is 45 cm². Find the value of x.

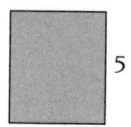

3 Solve these equations.

  a $3(x + 5) = 24$
  b $5(x - 2) = 35$
  c $4(10 - x) = 28$
  d $-2(x + 5) = -20$
  e $4(x + 4) = 8$
  f $7(2x + 4) = 4$
  g $3x + 2 = 6x - 2$
  h $5x - 3 = 3x + 3$
  i $9x + 4 = 12x - 11$
  j $3x + 7 = 5x + 4$
  k $7x - 4 = 3x - 21$
  l $2x - 4 = 5x + 3.5$

4 Write equations for these 'think of a number' problems and then solve each equation.

  a I think of a number, then multiply it by 5 and add 6. The answer is 21.
  b I think of a number, then multiply it by 4 and add 3. The answer is the same as multiplying the same number by 5 and subtracting 2.
  c I think of a number and add 6, then multiply it by 4 and the answer is 36.
  d I think of a number, then multiply it by 7 and subtract 5. The answer is the same as multiplying the same number by 3 and adding 3.
  e I think of a number and subtract 5, then multiply by 4 and the answer is -32.

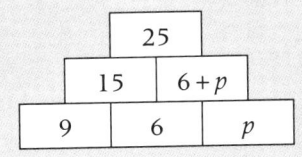

A5 HW4 Chapter review

1 Solve these equations.
  a $3x = 15$
  b $2x + 4 = -4$
  c $\frac{x}{3} + 3 = 6$

2 Solve these equations.
  a $4b + 3 = 15$
  b $20 = 5x - 2.5$
  c $\frac{x}{3} - 4 = 3$
  d $100 - 6x = 64$

3 Using algebra, write and solve these equations.
  a a number multiplied by 5 then 6 added equals 36
  b a number subtracted from 9 equals -3
  c 27 is equal to a number multiplied by 4 and 3 added.

4 Solve these equations.
  a $6b + 4 = 22$
  b $5f - 4 = 26$
  c $7f + 2 = 23$
  d $\frac{p}{4} + 3 = 12$
  e $9m - 12 = 42$
  f $\frac{r}{8} - 5 = -1$
  g $6d + 9 = 63$
  h $r - 12 = -2$
  i $6k + 4 = 19$
  j $3t + 5 = -13$
  k $\frac{f}{6} - 6 = -1$
  l $7p + 11 = -66$

5 The number in each brick is the result of adding the numbers in the two bricks beneath it.
By writing equations find the unknown letter in each wall.

a

	17	
	$4 + n$	$n + 3$
4	n	3

b

	25	
	15	$6 + p$
9	6	p

A6 HW1 Check-in review

1 James spent $\frac{1}{5}$ of his pocket money on a cricket set. He spent $\frac{1}{3}$ of his pocket money on a football. Work out the fraction of his pocket money he has left.

2 Calculate each of these, giving your answer in its simplest form where appropriate.

   a $\frac{1}{4} + \frac{1}{4}$ **b** $\frac{2}{9} + \frac{4}{9}$ **c** $\frac{10}{19} - \frac{4}{19}$

   d $\frac{4}{15} + \frac{6}{15}$ **e** $\frac{23}{28} - \frac{2}{28}$ **f** $\frac{4}{24} + \frac{14}{24}$

   g $\frac{17}{11} - \frac{6}{11}$ **h** $\frac{12}{7} + \frac{14}{7}$ **i** $\frac{17}{13} - 1$

3 Calculate each of these and leave your answer in simplest form.

   a $\frac{1}{3} \times \frac{2}{5}$ **b** $\frac{3}{7} \times \frac{1}{3}$ **c** $\frac{9}{10} \times \frac{4}{5}$

   d $\frac{3}{4} \times \frac{7}{9}$ **e** $\frac{5}{7} \times \frac{1}{4}$ **f** $\frac{1}{2} \times \frac{5}{9}$

   g $\frac{2}{3} \div \frac{3}{5}$ **h** $\frac{3}{7} \div \frac{5}{6}$ **i** $\frac{5}{12} \div \frac{4}{5}$

   j $\frac{4}{5} \div \frac{2}{3}$ **k** $\frac{9}{10} \div \frac{1}{8}$ **l** $\frac{3}{5} \div \frac{3}{7}$

4 Solve these equations.

   a $4n - 6 = 34$
   b $4f + 3 = -17$
   c $10 = 3x + 1$
   d $20 - 5x = -5$
   e $7d + 4 = -10$
   f $24 - 5k = 9$

A6 HW2   Equations and formulae

1 Substitute the values $a = 2$, $b = 3$, $c = \frac{1}{2}$ into each expression.

  a $4a + b$
  b $ac + 1$
  c $2b - a$
  d $6b + c$
  e $2a + b + 5c$
  f $3c + 2a - b$
  g $(a + b)^2$
  h $2a^2 - 2c$
  i $\frac{bc}{a}$
  j $3ab + 2bc$

2 Solve the equations.

  a $2x + 3 = 15$
  b $5a + 7 = 42$
  c $4m + 5 = 9$
  d $7p + 4 = 18$
  e $2(x + 1) = 12$
  f $4(2a + 2) = 32$
  g $12w - 7 = 10w - 1$
  h $3(2m - 1) = 5(m + 1)$

3 The voltage V in an electrical circuit, with current I and resistance R, is given by the formula

  $V = IR$

  a What is V when
   i $I = 6$ and $R = 8$
   ii $I = 8$ and $R = 12$?
  b What is R when $V = 56$ and $I = 8$?

4 The formula for the volume V of a cuboid is

  $V = lwh$

  where l = length, w = width and h = height.

  a Find the volume of a cuboid with $l = 5$ cm, $w = 2$ cm, $h = 3$ cm.
  b Which of these cuboids will give the largest volume?

   i $l = 4$ cm, $w = 5$ cm, $h = 2$ cm
   ii $l = 4$ cm, $w = 3$ cm, $h = 3$ cm
   iii $l = 5$ cm, $w = 1$ cm, $h = 7$ cm

A6 HW3 Writing formulae and changing the subject

1 Tickets for the cinema cost £4.50 for adults and £2.50 for children.

   a Write a formula for the total cost, C, for p adults and q children.

   The total cost of tickets for a group of adults and children to go to the cinema was £25.50.

   b If there were 3 children, work out how many adults went to the cinema.

2 The cost of hiring a cement mixer is £29 plus £5 for each hour.

   a Write a formula for the cost, C, to hire the cement mixer for n hours.

   b Use your formula to work out how much it costs to hire a cement mixer for 8 hours.

   c If the cost of hiring a cement mixer was £54, how many hours was it hired for?

3 Rearrange each formula to make a the subject.

   a $a + 4b = 10$
   b $4a - b = 12$
   c $6b + a = 20$
   d $b = \frac{a}{3} + 4$
   e $16 + 3a = 7b$

4 Jim's grandmother's formula for calculating the amount of cooking time, t, needed to roast a turkey is

$$t = 0.5w + 2$$

where w = weight of the turkey.

   a Rearrange the formula to make w the subject.

   b Using the rearranged formula, work out the weight of the turkey if Jim uses a cooking time, t, of

     i 3.5 hours
     ii 3 hours
     iii 5 hours.

A6 HW4 Inequalities

1 In these inequalities y is an integer.
For each inequality, write all possible values of y.
- **a** $-3 < y < -1$
- **b** $-5 \leqslant y < 2$
- **c** $4 > y > 1$
- **d** $6 < 2y < 10$
- **e** $-4 < 4y \leqslant 16$

2 a Write all the possible values of x in this inequality where x is an integer.

$-3 < x \leqslant 1$

b Show all the possible values of x on a number line.

Example

Show the solution set to the inequality $3x + 4 \leqslant 19$ on a number line.

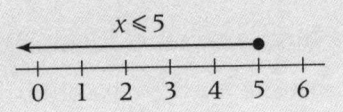

$3x + 4 \leqslant 19$
$3x \leqslant 15$
$x \leqslant 5$

$x \leqslant 5$

(number line from 0 to 6 with solution $x \leqslant 5$ shown)

3 Solve these inequalities and show the solution set on a number line.
- **a** $3x \leqslant 9$
- **b** $4x > 16$
- **c** $5x \geqslant 15$
- **d** $6x \leqslant 18$
- **e** $3x \leqslant -12$
- **f** $2x \geqslant -20$

4 Solve these inequalities and show the solution set on a number line.
- **a** $4x + 5 > 17$
- **b** $3x - 4 < 5$
- **c** $3x + 1 < -2$
- **d** $5x + 3 \leqslant 23$
- **e** $3x + 5 \geqslant 20$
- **f** $6x + 2 < -16$

A6 HW5 Chapter review

1 Whilst doing a science experiment, Sam is told to use the equation

$$v = 9.81t - 5.27$$

to work out the value of v.
She uses her calculator to work out the value of v when $t = 5.89$.

  a Work out the correct value of v when $t = 5.89$.
  b Rearrange the equation $v = 9.81t - 5.27$ to make t the subject.
  c Use the equation in **b** to work out the value of t when $v = 56.0425$.

2 Solve these inequalities and show the solution set on a number line.

  a $5x + 3 > 13$ **b** $8x - 4 < 0$ **c** $4x + 1 < -11$
  d $6x - 3 \leq 21$ **e** $2x + 5 \geq 22$ **f** $10x + 2 < -3$

3 In Greece a hire car costs €85 plus €30 a day.

  a Write a formula for the cost of hiring a car in euros.
  a How much does it cost to hire a car for 6 days?

G1 HW1 Check-in review

1. Write these numbers in order of size. Start with the smallest number.

   a 0.98, 0.9, 0.011, 0.646, 0.099

   b $\frac{3}{4}, \frac{3}{8}, \frac{1}{5}, \frac{6}{7}, \frac{7}{9}$

   c 0.45, $\frac{4}{7}$, 65%, $\frac{2}{3}, \frac{7}{9}$

2. Write a suitable estimate for each calculation. Clearly show how you estimated your answer.

   a 31.5 + 53.5
   b 778 − 615
   c 3.98 × 6.15
   d 29.85 ÷ 4.76
   e 79.98 × 4.21
   f 99.7 ÷ 5.15
   g $\dfrac{9.6 \times 4.7}{5.13}$
   h $\dfrac{69.7 \times 46.3}{19.6}$
   i $\dfrac{56.55 \times 3.14^2}{6.1}$
   j $\dfrac{(19.3 \times 1.98) + 9.8^2}{7.15}$

3. Sonia said, 'when $x = 4$, then the value of $3x^2$ is 48'.
   Trevor said, 'when $x = 4$, then the value of $3x^2$ is 144'.

   a Who was right? Explain why.

   b Work out the value of $5(x + 3)^3$ when $x = 2$.

4. Copy and complete the table of equivalent fractions, decimals and percentages. Write fractions in their simplest form.

Fraction	Decimal	Percentage
	0.5	
$\frac{1}{4}$		
		75%
$\frac{1}{3}$		
	0.125	
$\frac{4}{9}$		
		2%
	0.004	
$\frac{1}{13}$		
		8.5%

G1 HW2 Measures, perimeter and area

1 Convert these measurements to the units given.
   a 30 mm = ___ cm
   b 300 cm = ___ m
   c 3 kg = ___ g
   d 5000 ml = ___ litres
   e 0.5 km = ___ m
   f 6 litres = ___ ml
   g 4.5 t = ___ kg
   h 7 m = ___ cm
   i 30 cl = ___ litres
   j 0.25 cm = ___ mm

2 Convert these measurements to the units given.
   a 24 km = ___ miles
   b 85 miles = ___ km
   c 1.5 miles = ___ km
   d 20 km = ___ miles
   e 4 kg = ___ lb
   f 6.6 lb = ___ kg
   g 41 kg = ___ lb
   h 9.9 lb = ___ kg
   i 5 oz = ___ g
   j 90 g = ___ oz

   Hint: 5 miles ≈ 8 km, 1 kg ≈ 2.2 lb, 1 oz ≈ 30 g.

3 Calculate the area of these shapes. State the units.
   a square, 5 cm
   b rectangle, 3 mm by 7 mm
   c right-angled triangle, 4 cm and 2.5 m
   d triangle, height 5 cm, base 70 mm
   Hint: units!

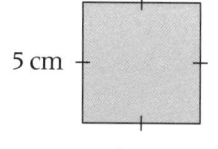

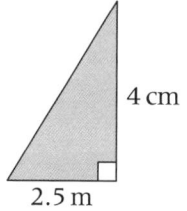

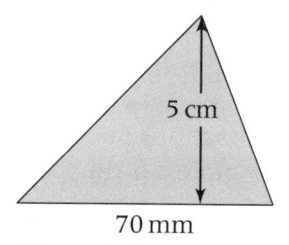

4 Calculate the perimeter and area of these shapes. State the units of your answers.
   a L-shape: 2 cm, 5 cm, 2 cm, 4 cm
   b U-shape: 3 m, 3 m, 4 m, 6 m, 8 m

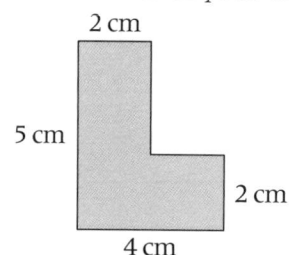

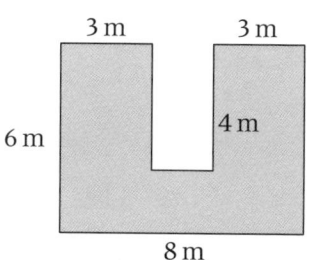

G1 HW3   Area and surface area

1 Calculate the area of these shapes. State the units.

a. 3 cm (height), 4 cm (base) — parallelogram

b. 5 mm (height), 6 mm (base) — parallelogram

c. 2 cm (top), 3 cm (height), 4 cm (bottom) — trapezium

d. 3 m (top), 5 m (slant side), 5 m (bottom) — right trapezium

2 The area of these shapes is given. Calculate the unknown lengths.

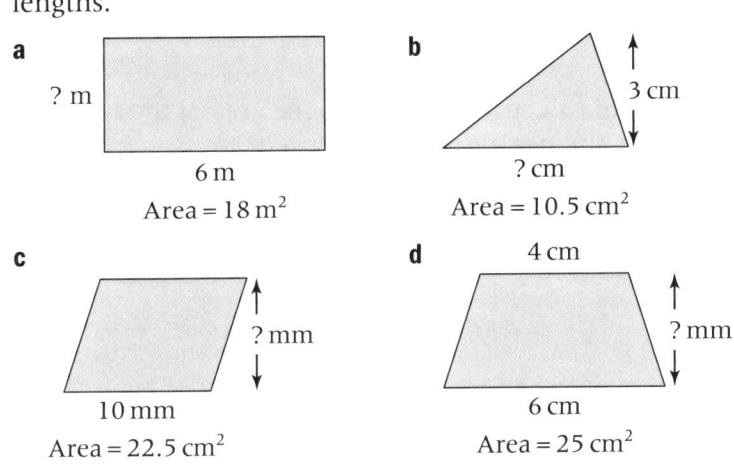

a. ? m (height), 6 m (base), Area = 18 m²

b. 3 cm (height), ? cm (base), Area = 10.5 cm² — triangle

c. ? mm (height), 10 mm (base), Area = 22.5 cm² — parallelogram

d. 4 cm (top), ? mm (height), 6 cm (bottom), Area = 25 cm² — trapezium

3 Calculate the surface area of these shapes. State the units of your answers.

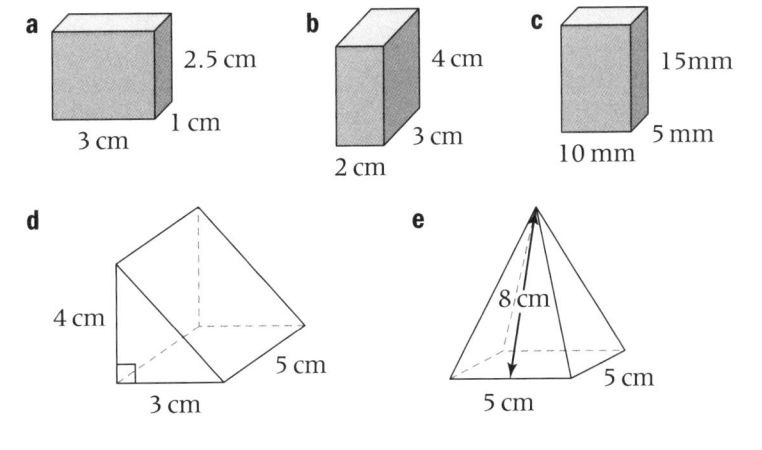

a. 2.5 cm, 1 cm, 3 cm — cuboid

b. 4 cm, 3 cm, 2 cm — cuboid

c. 15 mm, 5 mm, 10 mm — cuboid

d. 4 cm, 3 cm, 5 cm — triangular prism

e. 8 cm (slant), 5 cm, 5 cm — square-based pyramid

G1 HW4 Chapter review

1. Put these measurements in order of size, starting with the smallest.
   a 10 miles, 10 kilometres, 55 000 feet
   b 35 mph, 60 kmph, 45 mph
   c 12 inches, 29 centimetres, 1.2 feet
   d 4 pints, 4 litres, 400 ml

2. The diagram shows the shape of a classroom that will be covered in carpet. Work out the area of the carpet.

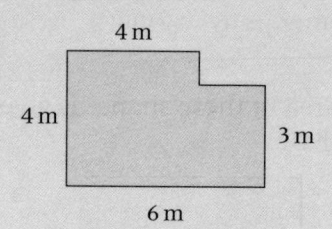

   4 m
   4 m
   3 m
   6 m

3. The area of this square is 4 times the area of the triangle. Work out the **perimeter** of the square.

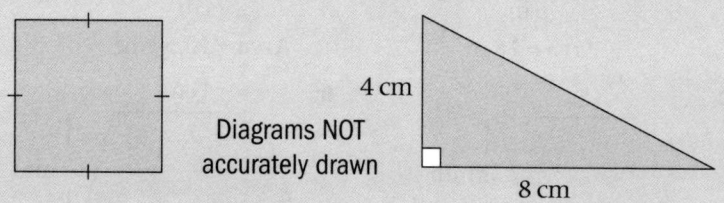

   4 cm
   8 cm

   Diagrams NOT accurately drawn

4. This is an open top tank in the shape of a cuboid.

   The outside of the tank needs to be painted.
   1 litre of paint will cover 3 m^2.
   The cost of the paint is £3.99 per litre.

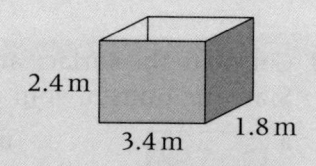

   2.4 m
   3.4 m
   1.8 m

   Calculate the cost of the paint needed to paint the outside of the tank. (If only part of a tin is used you must include the cost of the whole tin.)

5. These weights are given to the nearest kilogram. Give the lowest and highest weights they could represent
   a 3 kg   b 8 kg   c 15 kg   d 50 kg   e 0 kg

G2 HW1 Check-in review

1 a Expand these brackets.
  i $4(x + 5)$ **ii** $5(x + 3)$ **iii** $4(3 - x)$ **iv** $3(2x + 4)$
  b Factorise these expressions.
  i $3x + 9$ **ii** $5x - 20$ **iii** $12x + 6$ **iv** $4x + 8$

2 Calculate the area of each shape.
State the units.

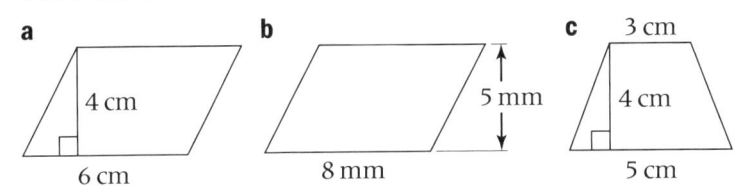

a 4 cm, 6 cm
b 5 mm, 8 mm
c 3 cm, 4 cm, 5 cm

3 The area of the square is twice the area of the triangle.
Work out the **perimeter** of the square.

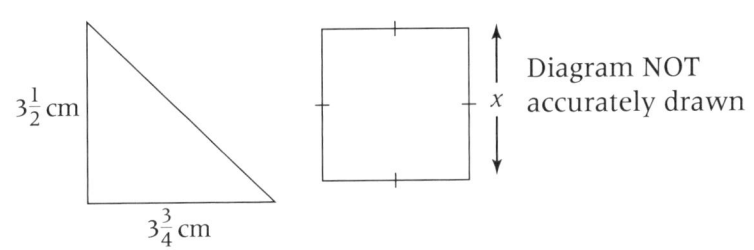

$3\frac{1}{2}$ cm, $3\frac{3}{4}$ cm, x

Diagram NOT accurately drawn

4 Simplify each of these expressions.
  a $\dfrac{b^4 \times b^3}{b^2}$ **b** $\dfrac{t^5 \times t^2}{t^5}$ **c** $\dfrac{m \times m^6}{m^2}$
  d $\dfrac{t^5 \times t^3 \times t^2}{t}$ **e** $\dfrac{n^3 \times n^6 \times n}{n^3}$ **f** $\dfrac{p \times p^2 \times p^2}{p^3 \times p}$

5 In each of these expressions $a = -4$, $b = 3$ and $c = -6$.
Calculate the value of these expressions.
  a $b + 5$ **b** $2b - 7$ **c** $a - b$
  d $b + 3c$ **e** $a + 2b + c$ **f** $a + b - 3c$
  g $4c - b - a$ **h** $c - 3a + b$ **i** $a \times b$
  j $b \times c$ **k** $ab + c$ **l** $3bc - a$

G2 HW2 Angles and triangles

1 Calculate the size of the angles marked by letters.

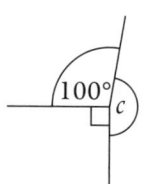

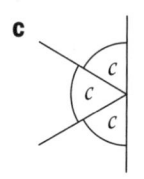

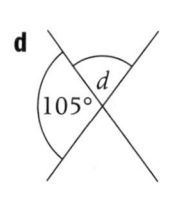

a 135°, a

b 100°, c

c c, c, c

d 105°, d

2 Calculate the size of the angles marked by letters.

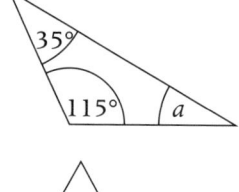

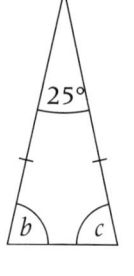

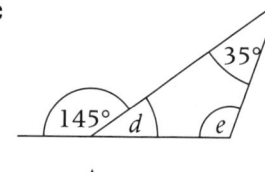

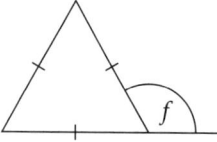

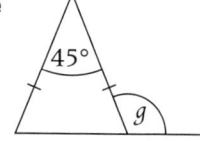

a 35°, 115°, a

b 25°, b, c

c 145°, d, 35°, e

d f

e 45°, g

3 Calculate the third angle of each of these triangles and state the type of triangle.

  a 35°, 100°
  b 45°, 90°
  c 15°, 120°
  d 60°, 60°
  e 27°, 143°
  f 75°, 30°

4 The points A (−3, 2) and B (−3, −4) are shown. Give the coordinates of a point C so that triangle ABC is

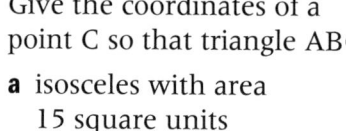

  a isosceles with area 15 square units
  b right-angled scalene with area 9 square units
  c right-angled isosceles with area 18 square units.

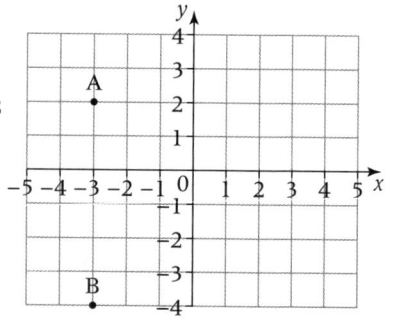

G2 HW3 Properties of quadrilaterals

1. Plot the points (1, 3) and (3, 1) on a copy of this grid. These points are two vertices (corners) of a shape. Using a different grid for each shape, add other vertices to make a
   a square
   b parallelogram
   c trapezium
   d kite.

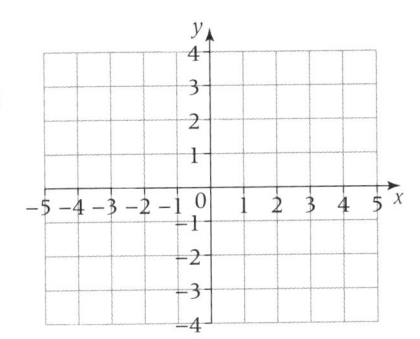

2. Work out the size of the angles marked by letters. Give a reason for each answer.

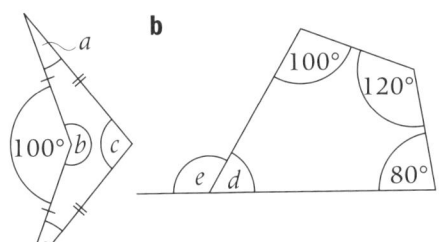

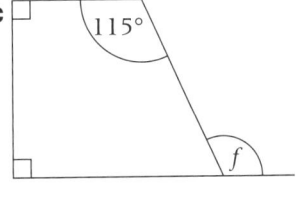

3. Calculate the value of x for each quadrilateral.

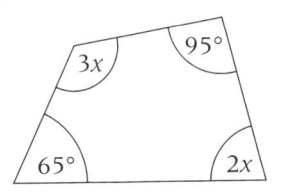

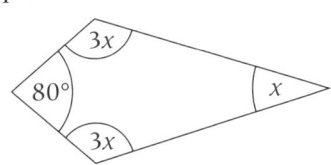

G2 HW4 Angles in parallel lines

1 Find the value of the angles marked by letters.

a

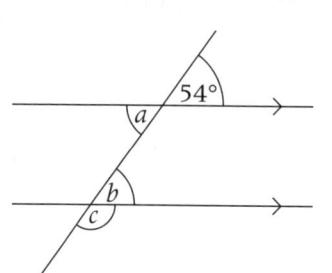

b

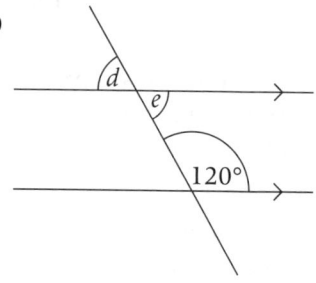

2 Find the value of the angles marked by letters.

a

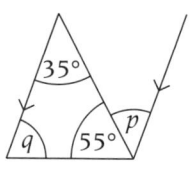

b

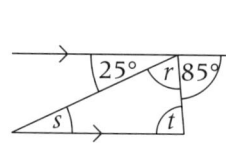

c

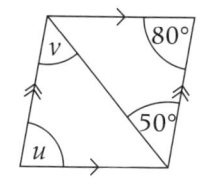

3 Use the diagram to prove that the angles of a triangle add up to 180°.

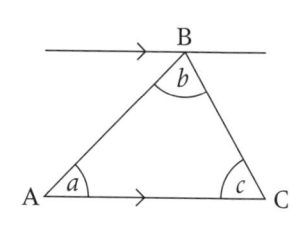

4 AB and CD are parallel.
Find the size of the angles marked
x and y.
Give reasons for your answers.

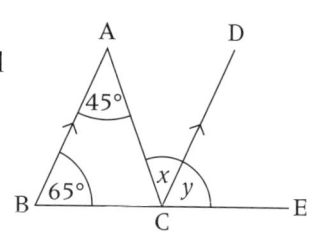

G2 HW5 Chapter review

1 Copy the table. For each of these shapes, put a tick in the box if the statement is always true.

Statement	Square	Rhombus	Trapezium
Diagonals cross at right angles			
Opposite sides are parallel			
Opposite sides are equal			

2 AB is parallel to CD.
Find the angle marked x.
Give reasons for your answer.

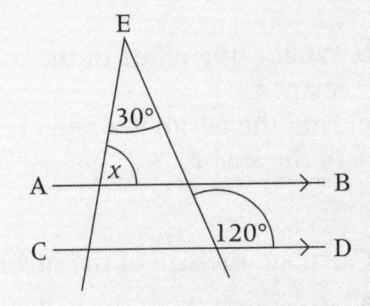

3 Copy the rectangle.

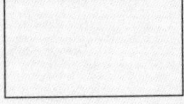

   a Draw all of the lines of symmetry on the shape.
   b Write the the order of rotational symmetry.

4 a Draw a circle with a diameter of 8 cm.
   b Draw a chord of length 6 cm inside the circle.

G3 HW1 Check-in review

1 Put these measurements in order of size, starting with the smallest.

  a 5 miles, 5 km, 6000 m
  b 1.5 kg, 1700 g, 1 tonne
  c 20 inches, 1 metre, 6 feet
  d 1000 mm, 1 m, 10 cm
  f 10 lb, 10 kg, 100 ounces

2 a Plot and join these points on a copy of the grid.
  $(-2, 2)$, $(3, 2)$, $(-3, -2)$, $(2, -2)$
  b What is the name of the shape?
  c Find the perimeter and area of the shape.

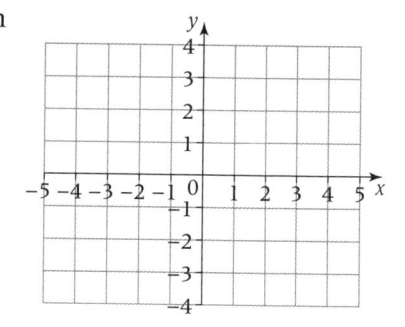

3 Calculate the size of the missing angles in each diagram.

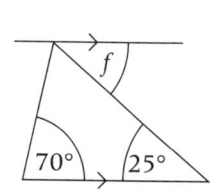

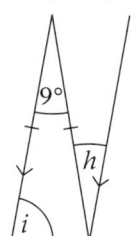

  a (angles 70°, 25°, f)

  b (angles 9°, h, i)

4 Expand and simplify these expressions.

  a $5(6 + x)$
  b $3(x + 4) + x$
  c $3(3x - 6) + 5x$
  d $7(3x + 2) + 6x + 2$
  e $7x(x^2 - 6)$
  f $5x(x + 2)$
  g $4x(x^2 - 2)$
  h $6x^2(x^2 + 5)$
  i $5(x + 3) + 7(x - 2)$
  j $5(2x + 6) + 6(x - 3)$
  k $3(5x + 6) - 6(x + 3)$
  l $3(5x - 2) - 3(x + 3)$

G3 HW2 3-D shapes

1 Write down the names of these 2-D and 3-D shapes.

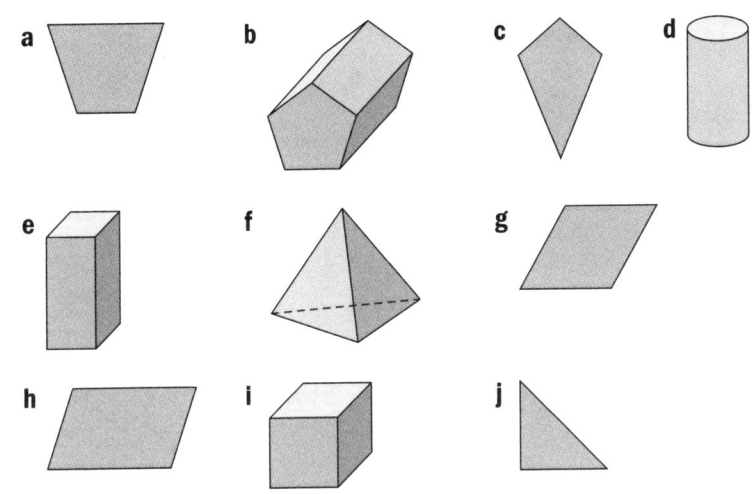

a   b   c   d

e   f   g

h   i   j

2 Draw the nets for shapes **b**, **d**, **e**, **f** and **i** in question **1**.

3 Which of these is the net for this cube?

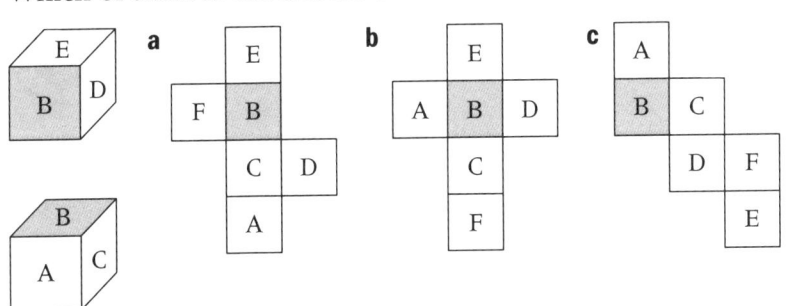

a   b   c

G3 HW3 Volume of cuboids and prisms

1 Using this formula work out the volume of the shapes.

Volume of prism = Area of cross-section × length

a Area = 4 cm², 7 cm

b 4 cm, 5 cm, 2 cm

c 6 cm, 5 cm, 12 cm

d 6 cm, 2 cm, 3 cm, 10 cm

2 a A cube has a volume of 216 cm³. What are its dimensions?
  b Between which two whole numbers does $\sqrt[3]{30}$ lie? Explain your answer.

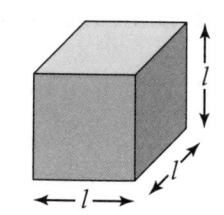

3 This is an open top tank in the shape of a cuboid.

The tank is going to be filled with sand. Work out the maximum amount of sand that the tank will hold.

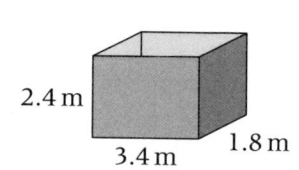

2.4 m, 3.4 m, 1.8 m

G3 HW4 Chapter review

1 Draw a sketch of the nets for these shapes.
   a cuboid 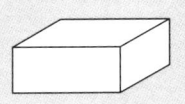
   b cylinder
   c triangular prism 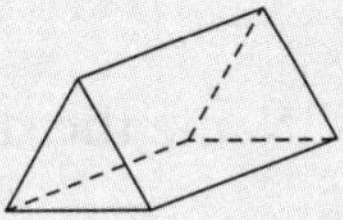
   d square-based pyramid

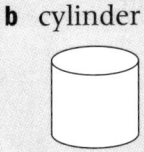

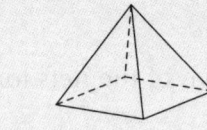

2 Calculate the volume of each cuboid.
   State the units in your answer.
   a 6 cm, 3 cm, 5 cm
   b 3.5 cm, 3 cm, 4.5 cm
   c 25 mm, 2 cm, 12 mm

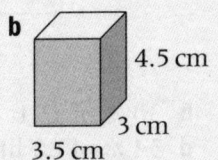

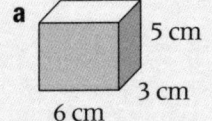

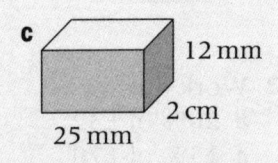

3 Water is stored in a tank in the shape of a cuboid with a square base.
   The sides of the base are 30 cm long.
   The depth of the water is 20 cm.

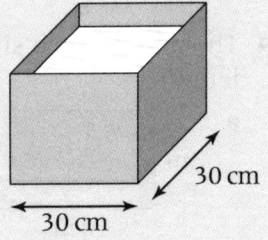

   a Work out the volume of the water, in cm³.

   More water is put in the tank.
   The depth of the water rises to 21.6 cm.

   b Calculate the percentage increase in the volume of water in the tank.

N7 HW1 Check-in review

1. Giving reasons for your answers, calculate
   a angle ABC
   b angle ADC.

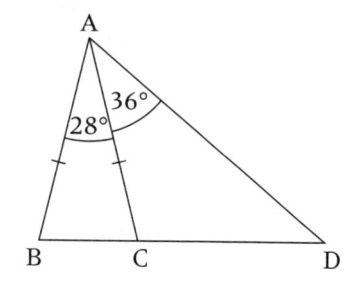

2. Draw a sketch of the nets for these shapes. Name the shapes.
   a 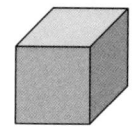
   b

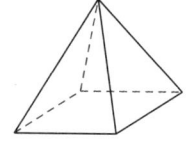

3. Work out
   a 20% of £32
   b 30% of £91
   c 15% of £70
   d 34% of 60 litres
   e 10% of 95 kg
   f 25% of 50 m

4. The area of each shape is given. Calculate the unknown length.

   a ? m, 6 m, Area = 24 m²
   b 5 cm, ? cm, Area = 40 cm²
   c 15 mm, ? mm, Area = 3.75 cm²
   d 5 cm, 7 cm, ? cm, Area = 48 cm²

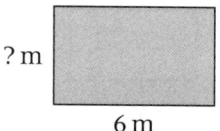

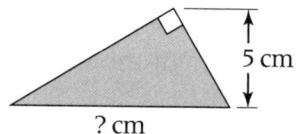

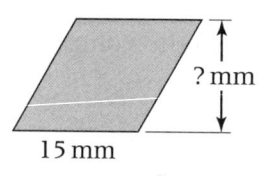

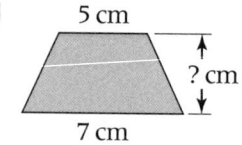

N7 HW2 Proportion and exchange rates

1 a Manjit cuts a piece of string into two pieces.
Piece A is 12 cm long and piece B is 16 cm long.

   i How many times longer is piece B compared to piece A?
   ii What proportion of the length of piece B is piece A?

b James is 8 years old and his Auntie Claire is 32 years old.

   i How many times older is Claire compared to James?
   ii What proportion of Claire's age is James' age?

2 Here is a recipe to make 8 shortbread biscuits.

150 g plain white flour   100 g butter
45 ml rice flour   50 g caster sugar

a How much caster sugar would you need to make 10 shortbread biscuits?
b Pam has 1 kg of plain white flour. She has plenty of the other ingredients. What is the maximum number of shortbread biscuits she could make?

3 Use this exchange rate to convert between each currency.
£1 = $1.84

a Convert these amounts of money into US dollars.
   i £55   **ii** £1000   **iii** £750

b Convert these amounts of money into pounds.
   i $250   **ii** $1500   **iii** $1 000 000

4 Sonia went skiing in France. She changed £250 into euros when the exchange rate was £1 = €1.44.

a Work out how many euros she received.

When she returned she had €125 left. The new exchange rate was £1 = €1.41.

b Work out how much Sonia got in pounds for her €125.

N7 HW3 Chapter review

1 Triangle ABC is similar to triangle PQR.
Calculate the length of

  a PQ
  b AC.

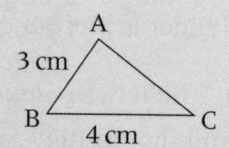

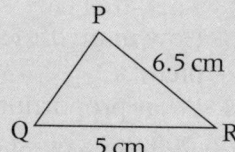

2 Jason fills a pool with 55 000 gallons of water.
He paid £128.70 for the 55 000 gallons of water.
Work out how much it would cost to fill a pool that holds 75 000 gallons of water.

3 Ayesha put £564 in a new savings account.
Simple interest of 4% was added to the amount in her savings each year.

Calculate the total amount in Ayesha's savings account at the end of 2 years.

4 Fred pays Income Tax at 22%.
He is allowed to earn £3500 before he pays any Income Tax. He earns £14 500 in one year.

Work out how much Income Tax he pays in that year.

5 Gemma invests £100 in a bank account.
Simple interest of 4% is added at the end of each year.
Work out how much money Gemma has at the end of

  a the first year   **b** three years.

6 Use a calculator to calculate these quantities

  a $\left(4\frac{4}{5}\right)^2$ **b** 2^8
  c $\sqrt{\frac{4}{9}}$ **d** $\sqrt[5]{243}$

G4 HW1 Check-in review

1 Complete these conversions.

   a ___ m = 670 cm
   b 3 km = ___ m
   c 1900 mm = ___ cm
   d 5300 g = ___ kg
   e 6700 ml = ___ litres
   f 9.5 litres = ___ ml
   g 9 tonnes = ___ kg
   h 14 kg 200 g = ___ g
   i 56 000 000 cm = ___ km
   j 0.009 tonnes = ___ g

2 For each of these 'think of a number' problems
   i write an equation ii solve the equation.

   a I think of a number, multiply it by 2, then add 4.
      The answer is 14.
   b I think of a number, multiply it by 6, then subtract 8.
      The answer is −10.

3 The number in each brick is the result of adding the numbers in the two bricks beneath it.
   By writing equations find the unknown letter in each wall.

   a
		24		
	?		?	
q	5		8	

   b
		32		
	?		?	
t		4		$3t$

4 Calculate these percentage increases or decreases without using a calculator.
   You must show all of your working.

   a Increase £250 by 10%
   b Decrease £400 by 25%
   c Decrease £60 by 17.5%
   d Increase 60p by 1%
   e Increase €300 by 15%
   f Decrease $320 by 35%
   g Decrease 80p by 65%
   h Increase $120 by 99%

G4 HW2 Reflections and rotations

1 Copy and complete the diagrams to reflect the shape in the mirror lines.

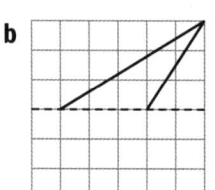

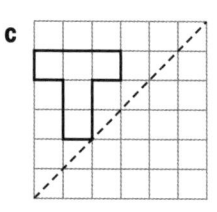

a   b   c

2 Give the equation of the mirror line for each reflection.

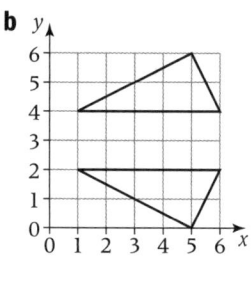

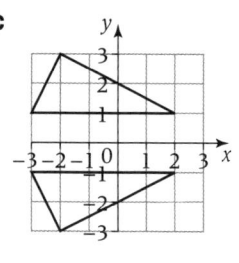

a   b   c

3 Copy the shapes onto squared paper. Rotate the shapes through the given angle and direction about the dot.

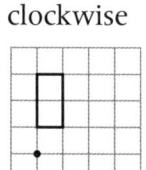

a 90° clockwise
b 180° clockwise
c 90° anticlockwise
d 180° anticlockwise

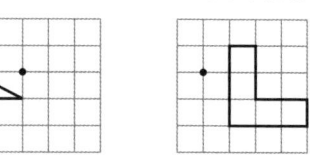

4 Copy the shape and grid onto squared paper.
  a Reflect the triangle A in the line $x = 1$. Label it B.
  b Rotate the triangle B by 180° about the point (1, 0). Label it C.
  c Describe the single transformation that maps triangle A onto triangle C.

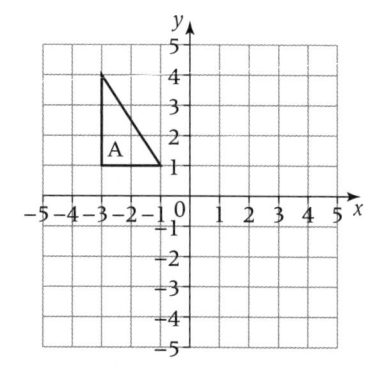

G4 HW3 Translations and congruence

1 Describe these transformations.
  a A to B
  b A to C
  c B to C
  d B to D
  e C to D
  f C to E
  g D to E
  h D to A

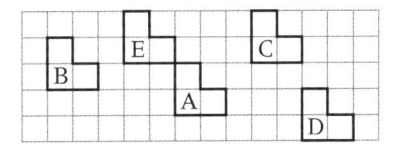

2 On squared paper, draw axes from −5 to 5 in x and y.
  a Plot and join the points (−3, 1) (−1, 1) (−1, 3) (−3, 4). Label it shape A. Name the shape.
  b Translate shape A by
    i $\binom{5}{1}$ Label it B.   ii $\binom{-1}{-5}$ Label it C.   iii $\binom{4}{-4}$ Label it D.

3 In each part, two out of the three triangles are congruent. Which are they?

  a i (70°, 45°, 5 cm)   ii (65°, 45°, 5 cm)   iii (45°, 70°, 5 cm)

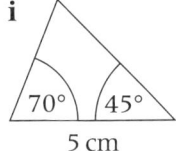

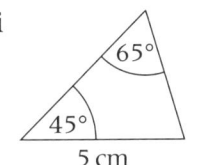

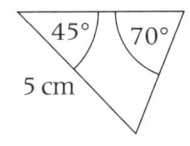

  b i (7 cm, 75°, 4 cm)   ii (4 cm, 75°, 7 cm)   iii (4 cm, 75°, 7 cm)

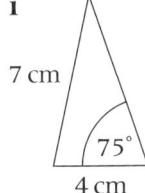

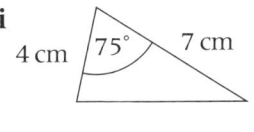

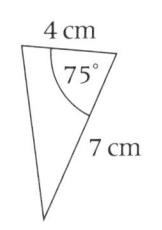

4 Copy the shape and grid onto squared paper.
  a Reflect the triangle A in the x axis. Label it B.
  b Rotate the triangle B by 90° clockwise about the origin. Label it C.
  c Describe the single transformation that maps triangle A onto triangle C.

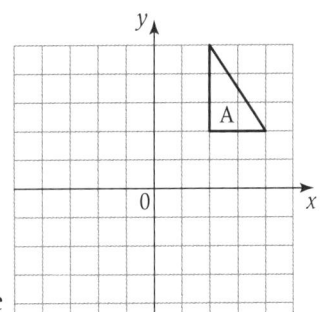

G4 HW4 Enlargements and similar shapes

1. Copy each diagram. Find the centre of enlargement and calculate the scale factor for these enlargements.
   The shaded shape is the original shape.

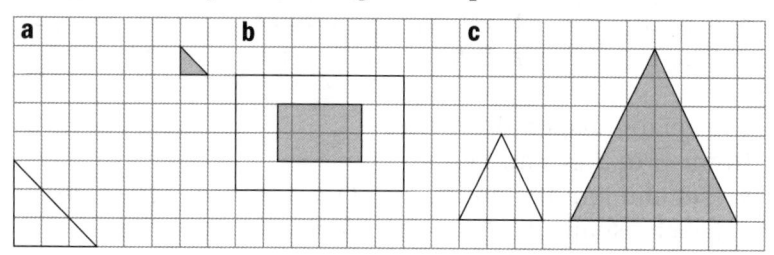

   a   b   c

2. Copy each diagram onto squared paper.
   Enlarge each shape by the given scale factor using the dot as the centre of enlargement.

   a Scale factor 3 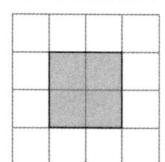
   b Scale factor $\frac{1}{2}$ 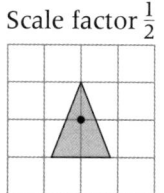
   c Scale factor 2

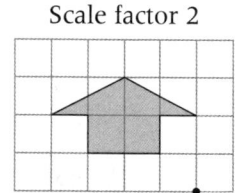

3. Calculate the unknown angle and find the two similar shapes.

   a 50°, 40°
   b 40°, 60°
   c 90°, 40°

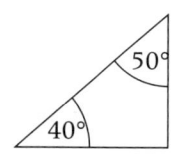

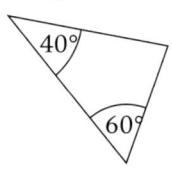

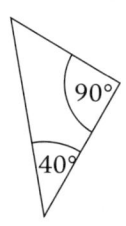

4. Calculate the value of the length marked by a letter.

   a 3 cm, 4 cm, 6 cm, a
   b 3 cm, 2 cm, 5 cm, b

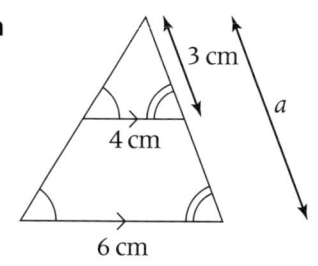

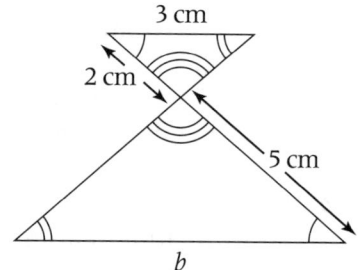

G4 HW5 Chapter review

1 Copy the grid and enlarge the triangle by scale factor 2 through the centre of enlargement (0, 0).

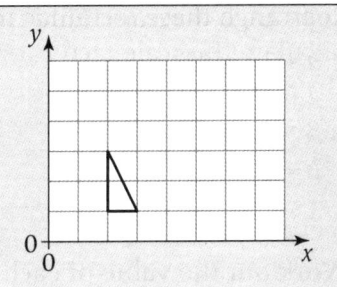

2 Copy the grid.
Shape A is rotated anticlockwise, centre (1, 0), to shape B.
Shape B is rotated anticlockwise, centre (1, 0), to shape C.
Shape C is rotated by the same angle anticlockwise, centre (1, 0), to shape D.

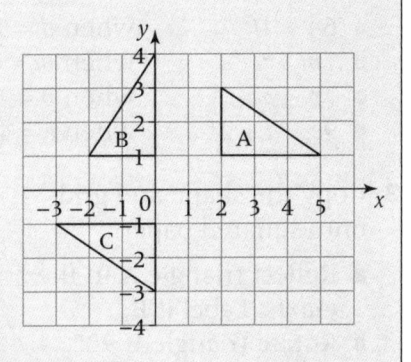

  a Mark the position of shape D.
  b Describe the single transformation that takes shape C to shape A.

3 Copy the grid.
The triangle R has been drawn on the grid.

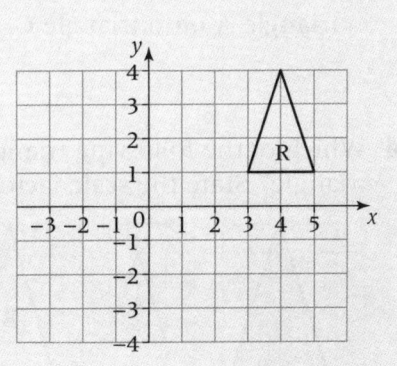

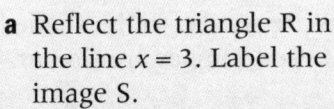

  a Reflect the triangle R in the line $x = 3$. Label the image S.
  b Rotate triangle S through 90° clockwise about (1, −1). Label it T.
  c Describe the single transformation that maps shape R onto shape T.

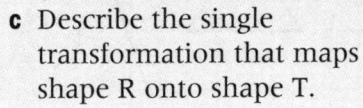

G5 HW1 Check-in review

1 Rearrange these formulae to make *a* the subject.
  a $a + 3b = 12$
  b $2a - 3b = 15$
  c $8b + a = 24$
  d $b = \frac{a}{5} - 5$
  e $15 - 3a = 6b$

2 Work out the value of each expression.
  a $6d + 4f$ when $d = 5$ and $f = 4$
  b $7m + n$ when $m = 4$ and $n = -5$
  c $7p - 3q$ when $p = 15$ and $q = -1$
  d $9e - d + 2f$ when $e = 4$, $d = -2$ and $f = \frac{1}{2}$

3 Copy the shape and grid onto squared paper.
  a Reflect triangle A in the *y*-axis. Label it B.
  b Rotate triangle B 90° anticlockwise about the origin and label it C.
  c Describe the single transformation that maps triangle A onto triangle C.

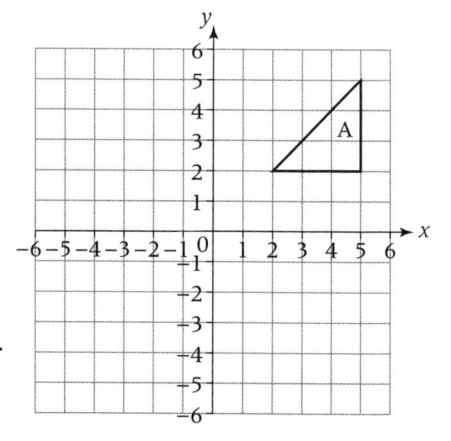

4 Which of the following triangles are similar to the shaded triangle? State the scale factor if the triangles are similar.

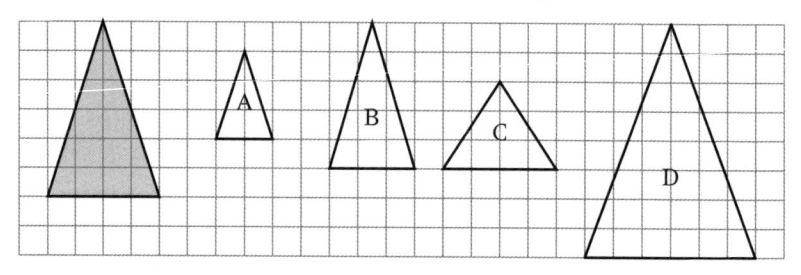

G5 HW2 Interior and exterior angles of a polygon

1 Calculate the sum of the interior angles of a

   a pentagon
   b hexagon   Hint: Split the shapes into triangles.
   c nonagon
   d decagon.

2 Calculate the size of

   i one interior angle
   ii one exterior angle

of a regular

   a quadrilateral
   b octagon   Hint: Exterior angles add to 360°.
   c heptagon
   d dodecagon.

3 The interior angle of a regular polygon is 120°.

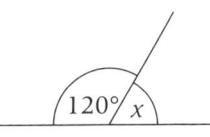

   a Calculate the size of the exterior angle x.
   b Calculate the number of sides of the regular polygon.
   c What is the mathematical name for this polygon?

4 A regular polygon has 20 sides.

   a Calculate the size of an exterior angle.
   b Calculate the size of an interior angle.

5 Calculate the size of the unknown angles in these polygons.

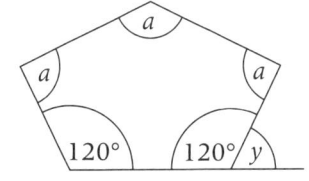

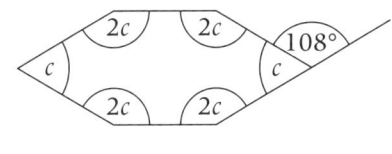

G5 HW3 Plans and elevations

1 The diagram shows a solid object.

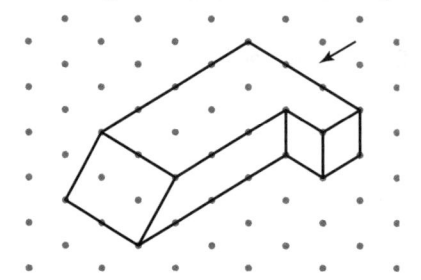

  a Sketch the side elevation from the direction marked with an arrow.
  b Sketch the plan of the solid object.

2 On squared paper draw
  i the plan **ii** the front elevation **iii** the side elevation
  of these solids.

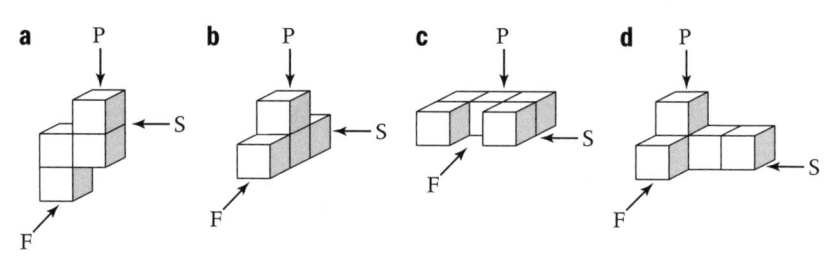

  a **b** **c** **d**

3 The plan and side elevation of a prism are shown.
The front elevation shows its cross-section.

  a On squared paper draw a side elevation of the prism.
  b Draw a 3-D sketch of the prism.

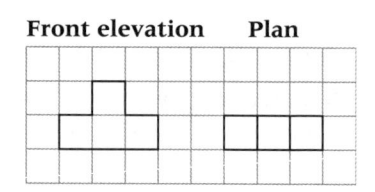

G5 HW4 2-D and 3-D measure; scale

1 Convert these areas to the given units.
  a $6 \text{ cm}^2 = \_\_\_ \text{ mm}^2$
  b $900 \text{ mm}^2 = \_\_\_ \text{ cm}^2$
  c $60\,000 \text{ mm}^2 = \_\_\_ \text{ m}^2$
  d $10 \text{ m}^2 = \_\_\_ \text{ cm}^2$
  e $9\,000\,000 \text{ m}^2 = \_\_\_ \text{ km}^2$
  f $6 \text{ km}^2 = \_\_\_ \text{ m}^2$

2 Convert these areas to the given units.
  a 5 cm^2 in mm^2
  b 500 mm^2 in cm^2
  c $50\,000 \text{ m}^2$ in km^2
  d 7 m^2 in cm^2
  e $7\,000\,000 \text{ m}^2$ in km^2
  f 7 km^2 in m^2
  g 4.5 cm^2 in mm^2
  h 950 mm^2 in cm^2
  i 4000 cm^2 in m^2
  j 5.25 m^2 in cm^2
  k $1\,200\,000 \text{ m}^2$ in km^2
  l 1.3 km^2 in m^2

3 a Convert these volumes to litres using $1 \text{ m}^3 = 1000$ litres.
  i 2 m^3
  ii 8 m^3
  iii 6.7 m^3
  iv 0.2 m^3

  b Convert these litres back to volumes in m^3.
  i 3500 litres
  ii 250 litres
  iii 20 000 litres
  iv 50 litres

4 This shape has a perimeter of 30 cm and an area of 39 cm². Calculate the perimeter and area of the shape after an enlargement of scale factor 3.

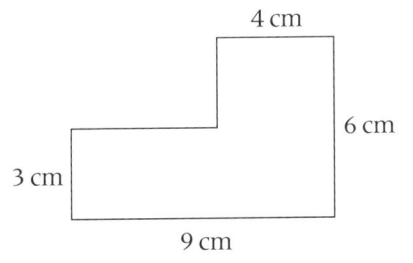

G5 HW5 Chapter review

1. The diagram below is part of a pattern. It is made up of a regular pentagon, squares and an isosceles triangle.
   a Write the size of the angle marked x.
   b Work out the size of the angle marked y.

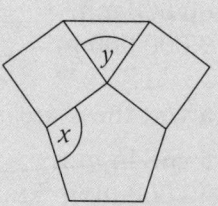

2. The diagram shows a solid object.
   a Sketch the side elevation from the direction marked with an arrow.
   b Sketch the plan of the solid object.

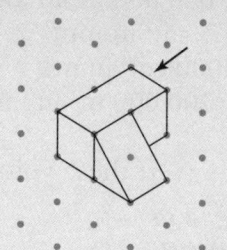

3. Here are the plan and front elevation of a prism.
   The front elevation shows the cross-section of the prism.
   a On squared paper draw a side elevation of the prism.
   b Draw a 3-D sketch of the prism.

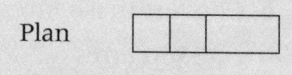

4. Convert these volumes to litres.
   a 4 m^3 b 10 m^3 c 0.3 m^3

5. Convert these areas to the given units.
   a 6 cm^2 in mm^2 b 7 m^2 in cm^2
   c 5000 cm^2 in m^2 d $3\,400\,000 \text{ m}^2$ in km^2

A7 HW1   Check-in review

1 Here is a recipe for bread and butter pudding:

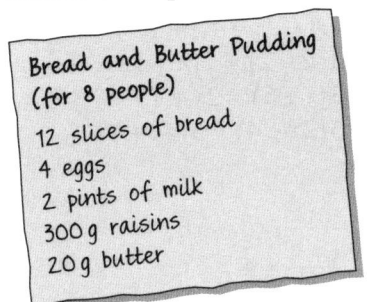

> Bread and Butter Pudding
> (for 8 people)
> 12 slices of bread
> 4 eggs
> 2 pints of milk
> 300 g raisins
> 20 g butter

Work out the amounts needed so that there will be enough for 6 people.

2 Express each of these as proportions. Give your answer as a fraction in its simplest form.
   a 50 kg as a fraction of 80 kg
   b £20 as a proportion of £50
   c 16 cm as a fraction of 64 cm
   d 450 cm as a fraction of 600 cm
   e 44 minutes as a proportion of 60 minutes
   f 540 metres as a fraction of 4 metres
   g 78p as a fraction of £2.

3 Use a protractor and compasses to construct these sectors of circles.

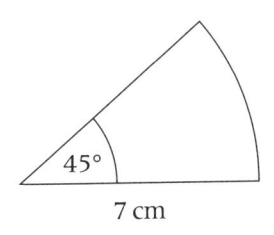

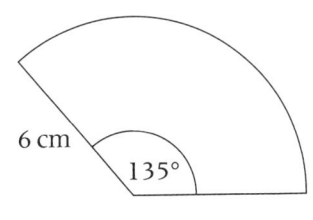

   a 45°, 7 cm

   b 6 cm, 135°

4 Copy the shapes and rotate them through the given angle and direction about the dot.

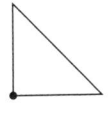

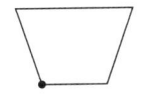

   a 270° clockwise

   b 90° anticlockwise

   c 180°

A7 HW2 Equations

1 Solve these equations.

a $2(b + 1) = 3b - 22$
b $5(f - 2) = 4(f + 1)$
c $2(k + 1) = 3k - 41$
d $4(u - 2) = 2(u + 10)$
e $4(v + 1) = 6v - 44$
f $3(x + 5) = 2x + 19$
g $5y - 10 = -4(y + 7)$
h $5(2x + 4) = 5(4x + 1)$

2 Solve these equations.

a $\dfrac{x+3}{2} = 4$
b $\dfrac{x+3}{5} = 4$

c $\dfrac{3x-6}{2} = 4.5$
d $\dfrac{3x-6}{6} = 4.5$

e $\dfrac{10-x}{2} = 3$
f $\dfrac{12-2x}{2} = 1$

g $\dfrac{3x+2}{2} = 4$
h $\dfrac{5x+2}{2} = -2$

i $\dfrac{3x-4}{13} = 2$
j $\dfrac{5-3x}{7} = 2$

3 In the two-way flow diagrams, find the starting number y that has to be input, so that you reach the same finish number F whichever route is followed. Formulate an equation to solve. The first one has been started.

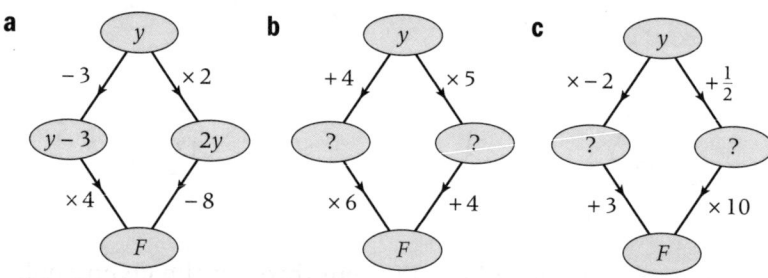

a (y → −3 → y−3 → ×4 → F ; y → ×2 → 2y → −8 → F)

b (y → +4 → ? → ×6 → F ; y → ×5 → ? → +4 → F)

c (y → x−2 → ? → +3 → F ; y → $+\tfrac{1}{2}$ → ? → ×10 → F)

Hint for **3a**: $4(y - 3) = 2y - 8$

4 Write two different equations that have a solution of $x = 3$. You should write one equation similar to question **1** and another similar to question **2**. Show your solutions.

A7 HW3 Finding solutions from graphs

1 a Draw the graph of $y = -2x - 3$ on a grid with axes from +10 to −10.
  b Use your graph to find
   i the value of x when $y = 9$
   ii the value of y when $x = -2$
   iii the value of x when $y = 0$
   iv the value of y when $x = 3$.

2 a Draw the graph of $2y + 4x = -10$ on a grid with axes from +10 to −10.
  b Which of these sets of points lie on the line $2y + 4x = -10$?

(5, −5)	(0, −5)	(−5, 0)
(−6, 7)	(7, −6)	(3, −1)
(−3, 1)	(1, 3)	(−1, −3)
(1, −7)	(−5, 5)	(−5, −5)

3 a Draw the graphs of the equations $x + 3y = 6$ and $4x + y = -9$ on the same grid with axes from +10 to −10.
  b Write the coordinates of the point where these two lines cross.

4 a Draw the graphs of the equations $2y = x + 9$ and $3y + 4x = 8$ on the same grid with axes from +10 to −10.
  b Write the coordinates of the point where the two lines cross.

A7 HW4 Chapter review

1 The equation $x^3 - 9x = 10$ has a solution between 3 and 4.
Use trial and improvement to find the solution to 1 decimal place.

Hint: Create a table to help you.

2 Match these graphs to their equations.

  a $y = 2x + 4$
  b $y = x^2$
  c $y = -3$
  d $y = x^2 - 4$
  e $y = -x + 3$
  f $y = -2x + 3$

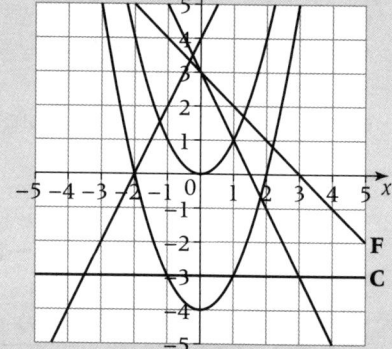

3 A rectangle has length 15 cm and width x cm.

  a Write a formula for the area of the rectangle.
  b Use an equation to determine x if the area is 135 cm².
  c Write a formula for the perimeter of the rectangle.
  d Use an equation to determine x if the perimeter is 78 cm.

4 a On a suitable grid, draw the graph of $y = 3x - 2$.
  b Use your graph to find
     i the value of y when $x = -2.5$
     ii the value of x when $y = 3$.

5 Solve these equations.

  a $\dfrac{x+4}{3} = 21$ **b** $3(5x - 6) = 147$

  c $\dfrac{2(x+6)}{3} = 6$ **d** $2x + 4 = 3x - 1$

  e $6(x + 1) = 14(x - 1)$ **f** $2(5x + 3) = 12x - 3$

G6 HW1 Check-in review

1 Complete these conversions.
   a 25 miles = ___ kilometres
   b ___ miles = 28 kilometres
   c 15 cm = ___ inches
   d ___ kg = 8.8 lb
   e 55 mph = ___ kmph
   f ___ litres = $14\frac{1}{2}$ pints
   g 20 cm = ___ feet
   h 30 g = ___ oz
   i 500 ml = ___ pints
   j 6 kg = ___ lb

   Hint: 5 miles ≈ 8 km, 1 inch ≈ 2.5 cm, 1 foot ≈ 30 cm, 1 kg ≈ 2.2 lb,
   1 pint ≈ 600 ml, 1 oz ≈ 30 g

2 Whilst doing a science experiment, Michelle is told to use the formula
   $$v = 9.91t + 5.45$$
   to work out the value of v.
   She uses her calculator to work out the value of v when $t = 6.78$.

   a Work out the correct value of v when $t = 6.78$.

   When $t = 8.26$ Michelle works out the answer to be 87.3066.
   Michelle's answer is correct.
   Michelle's friend Leah worked out v to be 23.62 when $t = 8.26$.

   b Suggest what is the most likely error made by Leah.

3 Copy and enlarge each shape by the given scale factor.

   a Scale factor 2
   b Scale factor 3
   c Scale factor 4
   d Scale factor 2

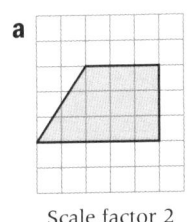

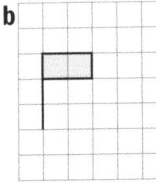

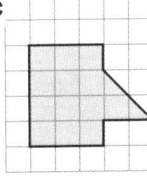

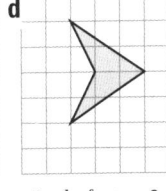

4 Triangle ABC is similar to triangle PQR.
   Calculate the length of
   a PQ
   b AC.

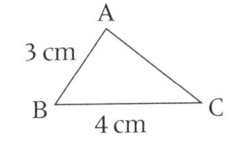

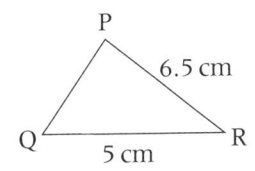

   Triangle ABC: AB = 3 cm, BC = 4 cm
   Triangle PQR: PR = 6.5 cm, QR = 5 cm

G6 HW2 Bearings and constructing triangles

1 A castle and church are on a small island.
A treasure chest is buried on the island.
The bearing of the treasure from the castle is 95°.
The bearing of the treasure from the church is 190°.
Copy the diagram of the island and mark the position of the treasure.

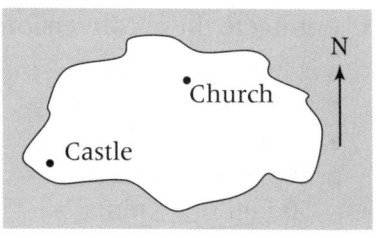

2 Use the diagram to measure the bearing of
  a Coventry from Birmingham
  b Worcester from Birmingham
  c Birmingham from Coventry
  d Worcester from Coventry.

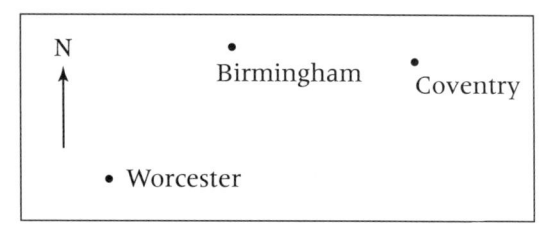

3 Make accurate drawings of these triangles.

  a SAS — 3 cm, 45°, 4 cm
  b ASA — 80°, 6 cm, 40°
  c SSS — 7 cm, 4 cm, 4 cm

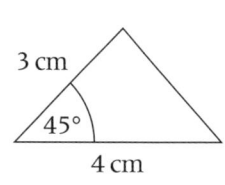

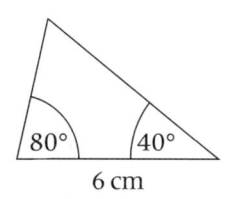

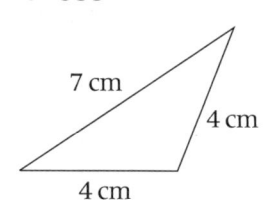

4 Make an accurate drawing of this net of a square-based pyramid.

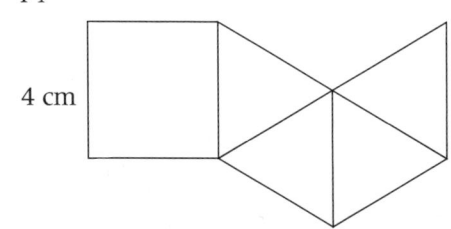

4 cm

G6 HW3 Perpendicular lines and angle bisectors

1 a Draw a line AB, so that AB = 12 cm.

A———————•———————B
　　　　　　P

b Mark the point P, so that AP = 8 cm.
c Construct the perpendicular to AB that passes through point P.

2 a Using compasses construct the triangle ABC.

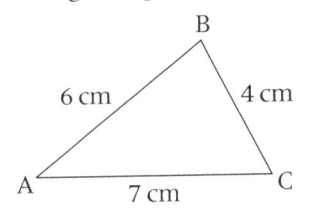

(Triangle ABC with AB = 6 cm, BC = 4 cm, AC = 7 cm)

b Construct the perpendicular bisectors of AB, BC and AC.
c Label the point of intersection of the perpendicular bisectors as O.
d What do you notice about point O?

3 Construct an equilateral triangle of side length 5 cm using only a ruler and compasses. You must show your construction lines.

4 a Using compasses, construct the triangle PQR.

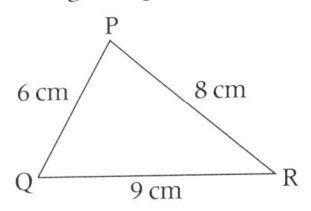

(Triangle PQR with PQ = 6 cm, PR = 8 cm, QR = 9 cm)

b Construct the angle bisectors for the angle P, angle Q and angle R.
c Label the point of intersection as O.
d Draw a circle, centre O, that just touches the lines PQ, QR and PR.
e State the radius of this circle.

G6 HW4 Loci and scale

1 Copy the line AB and draw the locus of the points that are always 2 cm from the line.

A ――――― B

2 Make an accurate copy of the points A, B and C. (You can use tracing paper.)

A •

• C

B •

Shade the region that satisfies all three of these conditions:

a Less than 2 cm from A
b Closer to AB than to AC
c Closer to A than to B.

3 A map has a scale 1 : 25 000 or 1 cm represents 25 000 cm. Calculate in metres the actual distance represented on the map by

a 4 cm
b 9 cm
c 7.5 cm
d 0.25 cm
e 12.5 cm

4 This is a sketch of the plan of a room. Make an accurate scale drawing of the plan using 1 cm = 50 cm.

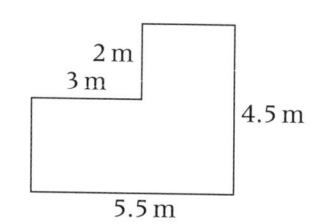

2 m
3 m
4.5 m
5.5 m

G6 HW5 Chapter review

1 Construct an accurate drawing of this triangle.

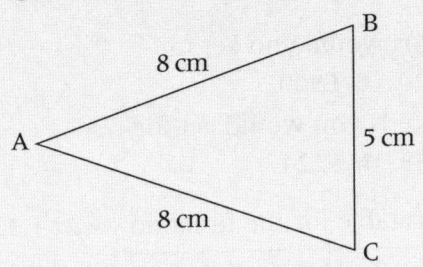

- AB = 8 cm
- BC = 5 cm
- AC = 8 cm

2 The triangle in question **1** represents a triangular garden ABC.
The scale of the diagram is 1 cm = 1 m.
A pond is to be built in the garden so that it is
  i within 4 m of point C
  ii equal distance from AB and AC.
On your triangle that you constructed in question **1**, use a cross to show the possible location of the pond.

3 This map shows the position of several cities and towns.

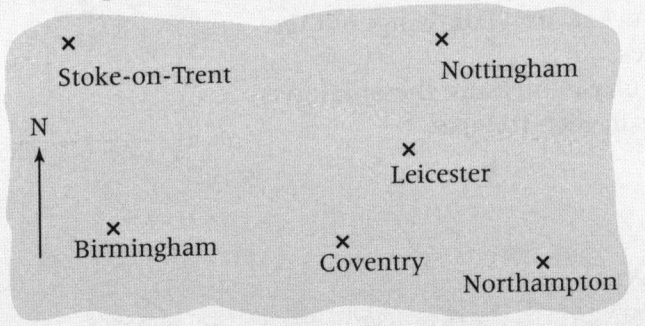

× Stoke-on-Trent   × Nottingham

N ↑

× Leicester

× Birmingham   × Coventry   × Northampton

Measure and write down the bearing of
  a Coventry from Birmingham
  b Northampton from Coventry
  c Stoke-on-Trent from Nottingham
  d Leicester from Northampton

G7 HW1 Check-in review

1 The exchange rate for euros to pounds is approximately
£1 = €1.40
Calculate how many euros would you get for
a £10   **b** £15   **c** £120   **d** £500
Calculate how many pounds you would get for
e €5.60   **f** €154   **g** €168   **h** €224

2 a Copy and complete this table for the function $y = 2x + 3$.

x	0	1	2	3	4	5
y						

  b On a copy of the grid, draw the graph of $y = 2x + 3$.
  c Draw the lines $y = 4$ and $x = 3$ on the same grid.
  d Use part **c** to solve these equations.
   i $2x + 3 = 4$
   ii $2x + 3 = 3$

3 Construct accurate drawings of these triangles.
Use a ruler to measure the unknown lengths in each triangle.

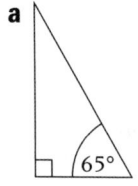

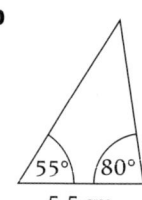

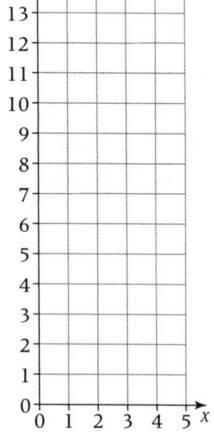

a 65°, 7 cm
b 55°, 80°, 5.5 cm
c 135°, 4 cm, 7 cm

4 The equation $x^3 + 4x = 198$
has a solution between 5 and 6.
Use trial and improvement to find this solution.
Give your answer correct to one decimal place.
You must show **all** your working.

G7 HW2 Circumference and area of circles

1 Calculate the
  i circumference **ii** area
  of each circle.

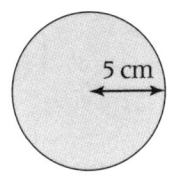

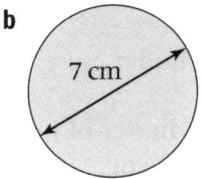

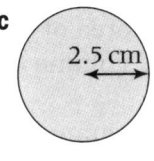

  a 5 cm **b** 7 cm **c** 2.5 cm

2 Calculate the **i** circumference, and **ii** area, of each circle.

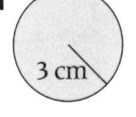

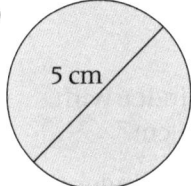

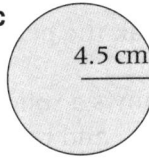

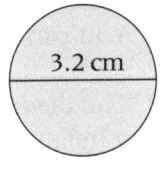

  a 3 cm **b** 5 cm **c** 4.5 cm **d** 3.2 cm

Hint: Circumference = $2\pi r$, Area = πr^2.

3 Using $\pi = 3.14$, calculate the radius of each circle.

  a Diameter = 6.3 cm
  b Circumference = 94.2 mm
  c Area = 50.24 cm^2
  d Area = 78.5 m^2

4 The diagram shows a semi-circle.
  The diameter of the semi-circle is 12 mm.

  Calculate

  i its area
  ii its perimeter.

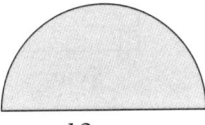

  12 mm

  Hint: A semi-circle is half a circle.

G7 HW3 Volume and Pythagoras' theorem

1 A cylinder of height 15 cm is shown.
The diameter of the circle is 5 cm.
Calculate

   a the area of the circle
   b the volume of the cylinder.

2 The diagram shows a cylinder of height
13 cm and a radius of 2.5 cm.
The length of a pencil is 14 cm.
Show that this pencil cannot fit inside
the cylinder.
You cannot break the pencil.

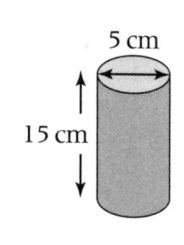

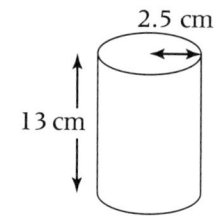

3 The diagram shows a solid cylinder with
a height of 12 cm and radius 5 cm.

   Calculate the volume of the cylinder.
Give your answer correct to
3 significant figures.

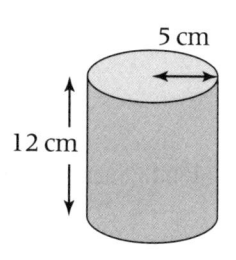

4 Calculate the length of the hypotenuse in
these right-angled triangles. Give your
answer to a suitable degree of accuracy.

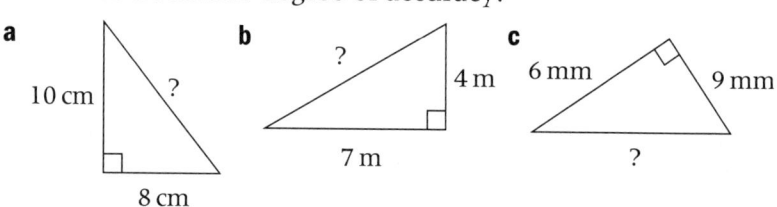

a 10 cm, 8 cm, ?

b ?, 4 m, 7 m

c 6 mm, 9 mm, ?

Hint: $a^2 + b^2 = c^2$

G7 HW4 More Pythagoras' theorem

1 Two right-angled triangles are placed together to form a triangle ACB.

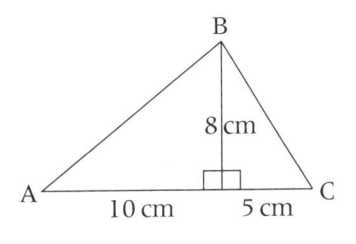

  a Calculate the length of AB.
  b Calculate the length of BC.
  c Calculate the perimeter of triangle ABC.
  d Is triangle ABC a right-angled triangle? Explain your answer.

2 Calculate the unknown length in these right-angled triangles. Give your answers to a suitable degree of accuracy.

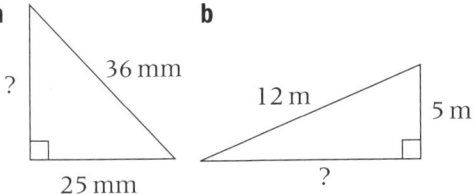

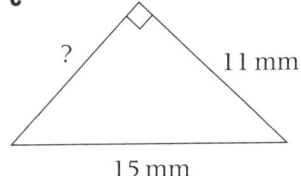

3 Calculate the perimeter and area of each shape.

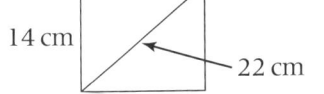

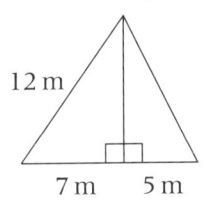

4 CD = 12 cm
BC = 7 cm
AB = 6 cm

  a Calculate the length of AD.
  b Calculate the area of ABCD.

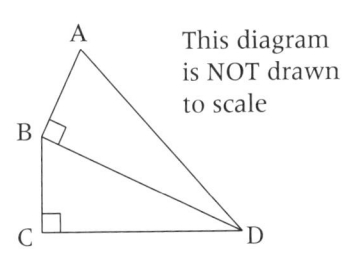

This diagram is NOT drawn to scale

G7 HW5 Chapter review

1 A cylinder of height 15 cm is shown.
The diameter of the circle is 6 cm.
Calculate
  a the area of the circle
  b the surface area of the cylinder.

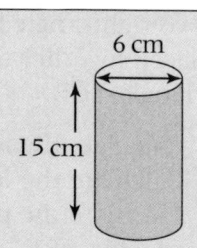

2 Using $\pi = 3.14$, calculate the radius of each circle.
  a Diameter = 5.6 cm
  b Circumference = 45 mm
  c Area = 153.86 cm^2
  d Area = 113.04 m^2

3 The diagram shows a cylinder of height 10 cm and a radius of 4 cm.
The length of a pencil is 12 cm.
Can this pencil fit inside the cylinder?
Explain your answer.

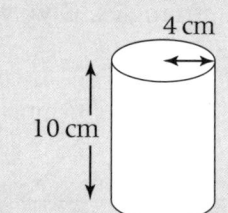

4 A cuboid has a square base of side length y cm.
The height of the cuboid is $(y + 2)$ cm.
The volume of the cuboid is 34 cm^3.
Show that $y^3 + 2y^2 = 34$.

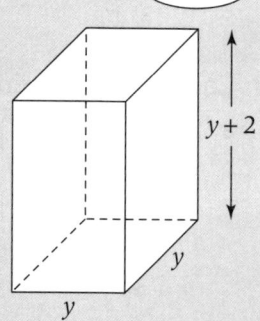

5 Copy and complete the table showing four journeys.

Person	Distance travelled	Time taken	Speed
Mrs Tomes	240 miles	3.2 hours	
Ms Howard	420 km	$3\frac{1}{4}$ hours	
Mrs Flynn	38 miles	20 minutes	
Mr Collins	10 km	12 minutes	